Other books by Kate Troyer

She Speaks
Shame Off You

Dear Kate

*Letters to Kate about Life, Love, and
Finding Happily Ever After*

Kate Troyer

WESTBOW
PRESS®
A DIVISION OF THOMAS NELSON
& ZONDERVAN

WestBow Press books may be ordered through booksellers or by contacting:

WestBow Press
A Division of Thomas Nelson & Zondervan
1663 Liberty Drive
Bloomington, IN 47403
www.westbowpress.com
844-714-3454

Scripture marked NIV are taken from the Holy Bible, New International Version®. NIV®. Copyright © 1973, 1978, 1984 by International Bible Society. Used by permission of Zondervan. All rights reserved.

ISBN: 978-1-6642-9256-7 (sc)
ISBN: 978-1-6642-9257-4 (hc)
ISBN: 978-1-6642-9255-0 (e)

Library of Congress Control Number: 2023902993

Print information available on the last page.

WestBow Press rev. date: 02/14/2023

I dedicate this work of my heart to Mom and Dad, who, for more than forty-seven years, through many life challenges, are still together. I am grateful to you both for showing me what it means to not give up on each other and for still saying I do, as many times as it takes, for as long as it takes. I honor you and give thanks that I have been given the gift of being your daughter.

ACKNOWLEDGMENTS

To my husband, the one who has chosen me time and again. I would not be who I am without you. For the gift you have been to my life, I am eternally grateful. You have my heart.

To my children, to say I am grateful that I was chosen to be your mama feels like an understatement. I am incredibly proud of you both. You are kind, thoughtful, strong, and wise individuals who have taught me a lot about life. I often give thanks to God for the gift you both are to me.

CONTENTS

PREFACE

Dear friend, within these pages you will find my heart. The journey to completing this book was much longer than I initially thought it would be. As with any creative venture we go on throughout our lives, this one was filled with bumps and bruises along the way. I am reminded anew that we discover who we are by inviting God to reveal his heart to us through each experience and by surrendering what we demand life looks like, beauty and grace are revealed in the unfolding of our experiences.

INTRODUCTION

Let me tell you a story about a little girl with brown hair and hazel eyes, who was timid in nature and would not talk to strangers, but who dreamed of growing up to marry a knight in shining armor who would love every little thing about her, and this love would put all the broken pieces of her heart back together. It turns out, her dream came true, and their love did just that. But first ...

CHAPTER 1

Knight in Shining Armor

He brought me out into a spacious place; he
rescued me because he delighted in me.
—Psalm 18:19, NIV

THE MORNING OF MY WEDDING DAY DAWNED WITH AN OVERCAST sky and an autumn chill in the air. A few crispy, faded-brown leaves clung stubbornly to bare branches. They rustled as the wind blew those that had already fallen across the parking lot of the faded red-brick church where I was to become the wife of a handsome young man who had asked me to marry him a little more than half a year before.

The hushed-but-excited buzz that went with just such events could be heard through the closed doors, behind which my bridesmaids and I prepared for the upcoming ceremony. Last-minute checks for loose thread on our dresses, stray hairs teased into place, and nervous laughter filled our room with awareness. We would soon stand before a congregation of three hundred wedding guests, taking part in the exchange of vows for this new life-changing journey I was beginning.

Soon, the wedding coordinator motioned for us to step through the open door and glide down the aisle as the wedding march rang out from the piano near the front of the sanctuary. The moment I dreaded had arrived: all eyes were fixed on me. With my parents at my side, I walked toward the man I would pledge to share the rest of my life with. I felt relief when I reached him and could turn my back on the many pairs of eyes taking it all in.

The ceremony began. The pastor shared a message on the merits of a godly marriage, followed by an invitation for my husband-to-be and I to step forward. We both agreed to the questions asked by the pastor, and after exchanging our vows, he presented us to the guests as husband and wife. The pianist played "Joyful, Joyful, We Adore Thee" as we walked to the back of the sanctuary—a big grin on my new husband's face, and a shy smile on mine.

After the last well-wishers exited the receiving line, we entered the reception hall and were announced as the newly wedded Mr. and Mrs. Troyer. Finding our seats at the head table, we were served punch, water, and plates filled with stick-to-your-ribs comfort food. My normally healthy appetite eluded me, but I managed to eat enough to silence the nervous hunger pangs while I sat, surrounded by the many beautiful people who had come to share this special day with us.

The flurry of activities ended with a series of photos taken outside, including a most embarrassing first kiss. My new husband and I left for Cleveland to begin our two-week honeymoon.

Nine months earlier, my dad had informed me that a young man had expressed interest in courting me when I turned eighteen—the age my dad had told me was an acceptable time to begin dating. I asked Dad who the young man was, but he simply instructed me to wait until I turned eighteen to find out. I stewed over this new bit of life-altering news, and with a quiet realization, I knew who it was. I went to my dad and exclaimed that if the person was Ivan Troyer, I was not interested. Dad simply encouraged me to wait and see.

Ivan was a handsome, good, hardworking young man whom many young women were interested in. Anyone would have been lucky to have him, but I had dreamed of falling in love—the head-over-heels kind—before getting married. I was not in love with Ivan. I had known him all my life and cared for him deeply, but I just could not see myself spending the rest of my life with him. The next few months passed by quickly as I pondered my future.

The morning after my eighteenth birthday arrived, and while finishing morning chores, Dad informed me that Ivan had asked for permission to court me. I told Dad that I wanted a week to think about it before I gave an answer. I knew I would eventually say yes, but on that day, I decided to drive the four hours to my best friend's house for the weekend. She had moved to a new community a few months earlier, so I would not have to face Ivan until I was ready to give him my answer.

Explaining how I knew I would say yes will sound strange to you. I knew that the ministers of our church had blessed the union and that my parents loved Ivan and were in full support of it. Thus, I decided that God must have been in support of it too. I also did not want to refuse Ivan, because he had left the Amish community at the same time my family had. After being disinherited by his parents, my family became his. I knew it would be quite awkward during all the family functions together in the future, knowing he loved me and wanted to marry me, if I chose not to say yes. I did not want to be the cause of that awkwardness.

I have often felt sad for my husband because of the way our relationship began. Who would want to marry someone who had chosen them by default? He deserved so much more than that, but so our story began. It was only after reading my first book, *She Speaks*, that my husband realized what my experience was like during the beginning of our relationship. It was a difficult revelation for him.

As you may have noticed, in my youth, I was the type of person who went through life with tunnel vision. It allowed me to see only what was directly in front of me. To see further overwhelmed me. I took life as it was handed to me, never thinking to ask myself what I wanted out of it.

As it turns out, God guided me in more ways than I was aware of. Many of the life decisions I made have worked out beautifully, despite my challenge to see these major life choices clearly in the moment.

Arriving in Cleveland after our long wedding day, we decided to go for a walk after getting settled into our room. The mild November weather allowed for a peaceful stroll around the motel parking lot at dusk. We were quietly comfortable in each other's presence, yet butterflies fluttered in my belly as I thought about the physical and most intimate part of marriage. Having not so much as held hands during our courtship, to consider giving my body to my new husband was exciting and a bit scary.

Thankfully, I had bought an informative book—*The Act of Marriage* by Tim and Beverly LaHaye—from our local Christian bookstore a few months earlier. It explained what a healthy relationship between a husband and wife should look like and what I should expect.

> Dear Kate,
>
> I highly recommend a woman educate herself about the act of marriage. Many men are not taught how to please a woman—by no fault of their own. It is just not an area most of us are taught the importance of. When women learn about this part of the relationship, their husbands can learn what a woman wants and needs along with them.
>
> Some are aware that women can enjoy the act of intimacy every bit as much as men. It requires patience and gentleness by the husband, especially when the woman has experienced trauma where her body has been violated. By taking the time to win his wife's trust, he will be rewarded with a deeply fulfilling and fun relationship with his wife, which will spill out into other areas, improving the relationship.
>
> Unfortunately, what some men know about the act of intimacy might come only from suggestive pictures and pornography, which depict this act very differently than in a healthy, loving relationship between a husband and wife. Pornography is attached to shame. One feels guilt and the need to hide it from others, thus staining the act that was created and designed by

God to be a sacred and safe exchange between a man and woman.

When men feed on pornography, it affects how they see women. Often without realizing it, they view women as objects, and this changes how they treat them. It is an incredible gift when a man views the act of intimacy without shame. It will allow him to see another woman and appreciate her beauty but not want to undress her with his eyes.

Men were designed to notice and appreciate the beauty of women. It is a natural thing. It is only when this appreciation is accompanied by guilt that the man feels ashamed for noticing and the woman in his life is negatively affected.

I feel deeply grateful that my husband feels free to notice when a beautiful woman walks by. He appreciates her beauty, just as I do, but he is respectful not to stare, which would make me feel disrespected and uncomfortable. His openness allows me to feel comfortable that, although he may look at a beautiful woman, he is not fantasizing about being with her. He does not feel guilty for appreciating beauty; thus, it sets us both free and makes me feel safe.

I share the above examples to encourage you to be open and direct with your husband. When we believe the act of marriage is something to be ashamed of, not talked about, we miss a beautiful part of God's design for marriage—that of safety and protection for each couple's journey together. A healthy relationship is a major investment in protecting each other from the desire to stray from the marriage.

Love, Kate

As we discussed the day of our joining, I began to come back down to earth, and emotions bubbled to the surface. Tears rolled down my cheeks that I thought would never cease.

Overwhelmed by my emotions, words refused to form, and my lips quivered too much to speak coherent thoughts. My sweet new husband held me in his arms, stroking my face, tears coming away wet on his hands. Kissing my cheeks with a tenderness I did not feel deserving of, he waited patiently as though sensing I needed more time.

I cannot effectively express to you how sweet a gift it was to realize I felt completely safe with my new husband. Ever since childhood, I had felt uncomfortable for anyone to get too close to me physically, but there was a gentleness to him that allowed me to let down my guard for the physical aspect of our relationship. I feel a profound sense of gratitude for this.

On an emotional level, I wanted to be loved with all my husband's heart, but I found it difficult to believe myself worthy of such love. I saw myself as a flawed, too-fat, too-silly, eighteen-year-old to be an equal to my husband, who already had life experience and who had turned thirty just two weeks before our wedding.

Today, I realized I was not a fat eighteen-year-old, as I harshly judged myself to be. The self-loathing I felt toward myself evokes sadness for the younger me, and if I could, I would tell her she was beautifully and wonderfully made.

I wanted my husband to tell me I was beautiful, but when he did, I did not believe him. The belief that I was not enough ran deep. Throughout my life, when I received a compliment from a stranger, friend, or acquaintance, I would try to shrug it off because I was convinced they were just being nice.

After refusing compliments a few separate times, I recognized I had offended a few people by not accepting their sincere compliments. I proposed in my heart to be gracious and accepting in the future when people expressed their opinion and simply to say thank you.

The next day began early with our flight to Los Angeles, California, leaving at seven thirty in the morning. After holding my new husband's hand for the duration of the nonstop flight, I looked down where we were linked together and realized my hand no longer felt like my own; mine was soft, his was callused. Our two-week honeymoon had begun, and adventure awaited.

Over the next few days as we explored California, Las Vegas, the Grand Canyon, and other places, the vast age difference between us was glaringly obvious. I felt my husband's frustration in response to my silliness at times. He has a playful nature too, but with differences in what each of us found funny and with little in common, after a week, there were moments when we found ourselves wishing to return home. Alas, our return tickets were still a week away.

During our adventures, we got snowed in at the bottom of Glacier Park at Izaak Walton Mountain Inn and received a speeding ticket in the wide-open spaces of Nevada since my new husband wanted to test the Cadillac's mettle. We had rented a vehicle for the drive from state to state, and at a small family diner in Billings, Montana, we sat next to an interesting character who had us chuckling with his antics, and for years to come, my husband imitated him, resulting in generous giggles from me.

I am quite sure my husband married me in part because I laugh at all his jokes. To this day, he tries to make me laugh daily, and he always succeeds.

I appreciate him for bringing humor to our relationship since I am a seeker and a reader. I love to learn and discover new things, and I tend to be more serious. It is good to have a partner who, through his love for laughter, gifts me with the reminder to be in the moment, causing me to crack up sometimes when I would rather be serious.

Returning home, I walked into my parents' house, where I was quickly surrounded by my little sisters who wanted to hear all about my recent travel adventures. Everything felt different. The scents and sounds of the old farmhouse that had been my home for the past nine years were now a memory. I felt the change. It was time to create a home in a new space, one of my own, along with my new husband.

CHAPTER 2

Falling in Love

Love is patient, love is kind, it does not envy, it
does not boast, it is not proud. It does not dishonor
others, it is not self-seeking, it is not easily angered,
it keeps no records of wrongs. Love does not delight
in evil but rejoices with truth. It always protects,
always trusts, always hopes, always perseveres.
—1 Corinthians 13:4–7, NIV

LET ME TELL YOU ABOUT A TALL, LIGHT-BROWN-HAIRED YOUNG
man who walked up to my dad a few years earlier, next to where
we stood after the church service was concluded, and, with an
excitable voice, introduced himself as a man who had just recently found
freedom from his struggles in life by meeting God personally.

I had never seen him before, but I was at once drawn to him and
wanted to know more about him. Being the shy, soon-to-be fifteen-
year-old I was, I did not utter a word. I simply looked on, in my white
Amish Kapp and favorite royal blue dress, as the animated conversation
flowed around me.

The following day, in our farmhouse kitchen, I asked my mom
about the young man, and discussed my growing interest in him over
the next year. My dad encouraged me to put these dreams on a shelf for

the next few years. I sensed that he did not approve of my first newfound love interest. Today, I realize that my dad, who had more life experience than I did, might have noticed something about this young man that made him uncomfortable, something that I, as a young, impressionable young woman, might have been unaware of.

After having visited a revival meeting in our neighborhood, my parents were wading through the first steps of leaving the church of their youth with their large family of nine children, although we all still wore our Amish clothes.

To me, this expressive young man was larger than life. Over the next few years, as we periodically visited the "sister church" of the one we joined after we left the Amish community, participating in youth events and church conferences a few hours away, my love for the light-haired young man grew to dizzying heights. I dreamed of a future with him, for surely, he was to become my husband.

I did not talk to him often or much at all when I did see him, since I was instructed by Dad not to date until I turned eighteen. Soon after my sixteenth birthday, while visiting his home church again, one of the girls from the youth group asked me what I thought about the newly paired couple who had just begun courting. I tried to hide my shock as she confirmed that the couple included my light-haired young man.

It was a Saturday evening, and the conference was to continue the following day. Staying at the home of one of the church members, I held my composure, smiling as if on cue. I waited desperately for bedtime so I could take off the mask I was wearing. After the lights went out, I allowed the pain to flow through me. I tried to cry, and I tried to pray, but nothing came. If I could have been out somewhere that no one could hear me, I am sure I would have wailed, for words failed me. I tossed and turned and tiptoed to the bathroom repeatedly to put distance between my friend and me, not wanting to disturb her sleep, but I returned to bed each time and simply lay with the all-consuming pain. my heart was rent in two.

I sat through the conference the next day, smiling when needed but having little to say, waiting for the comfort of my own bedroom where

I could finally fall apart. As my dad pulled our big van into our family's hundred-year-old farmhouse driveway, I hurriedly ran for the safety of my room. There, as I buried my head into my pillow, the tears began and flowed until there were none left. Over the next two days, in the space where my heart had previously thumped contentedly, now there was naught but an indescribable physical ache.

I stumbled through the work week, trying to adjust to life without the promise of a future with my light-haired young man. Now, all that remained was the hope that his new courtship would end, and he would change his mind, realizing I was his intended.

As you can guess, when his wedding day arrived and he got married, I knew it was over and I had to turn my heart elsewhere, knowing it was wrong to have feelings for someone else's husband.

May I be frank with you in this moment? I have felt intense sadness over the fact that I married my husband by default. I felt guilty for his sake because I said yes to him in part because it would have made life awkward since my family had also become his family. In the first few years of our marriage, I struggled with feelings of betrayal because no adult in my life asked me if I was sure I wanted to be this man's wife. The church leaders wanted it, and my parents were happy with it, so what was not to like?

The bottom line is, I could blame others, but if I am honest with myself, I said yes because I thought God, my parents, and the church wanted me to marry him. I also allowed that to help me say yes because it meant I did not have to admit that I could have taken personal responsibility to say no.

Knowing I married my husband by default has affected my life dramatically over the years. I kept feeling like it was not God's will to have married him; therefore, upon reflection a few years ago, I realized that I had, in some ways, always had one foot out the door in our relationship. I was unaware of just how much this belief kept me from blooming where I found myself planted.

I have been the type of person who lets life happen to me instead of realizing that I get to choose. If I make God responsible for everything that happens in my life, it allows me to shrug off responsibility for my choices.

I was created with a will to choose. When I passed it off on God, it allowed me to be a passive bystander in my own life. Many days went by without carrying out meaningful things because I was waiting for God to drop my life's purpose into my lap.

It was quite convenient to hold a belief that supported me in being a casual observer of life instead of being an active participant. It was convenient to feel like a victim when it felt I was imprisoned at times. It was easy to blame God or others for a lack in my life, but if I am honest, my deeply ingrained and flawed beliefs had much more negative impact on how I experienced life than it would have, if I had chosen to be intentional with the opportunities and choices I was presented with throughout much of my life.

It is a sobering yet inspiring thought to realize that since I was born with a will to choose, the path my life takes is in direct relation to the day-to-day decisions I make. Where I put my thoughts, things grow. Therefore, what I think about daily affects my choices and the whole outcome of my life.

I have often heard people tell of God speaking clearly to them in some form about what their lives' callings are. For me, direction came with the quiet realization that what I was good at and interested in had the potential to be my life path to follow and to create with.

A few years ago, while spending quiet time with God, with a small amount of frustration, I asked him, "how do you see me?" I at once saw a picture of Jesus standing off to my side. His slightly longer-than-shoulder-length hair lay against the soft white cloth enveloping his body, and his hand rested on a shepherd's staff as he looked off into the distance. It was as if he was waiting for me. I understood him saying he trusts me with the journey and is walking right next to me. Tears of surprise and gratitude rolled down my cheeks as I pondered this experience.

There have been several times throughout my life when God has shown me pictures or visions of things relevant to my life in the moment. I remember reading throughout the Bible about times when people had visions or were visited by angels, but I did not expect this to happen to me because of the teachings of my youth. To say I was surprised when it happened is definite; but if I am honest, I ask, why would those things not happen since we get to have a living, breathing relationship with the one whose creation we are and with the one whose blood runs through our veins?

Dear Kate,

Did I ever tell you about the time I heard God's voice audibly? Each time I recall this experience, I am transported back to a small, dimly lit room with brown panel walls and just enough space for about fifteen chairs.

As I sat behind a window of glass, watching my son practice his martial arts class, I was feeling especially alone, and my heart was looking to know God in a deeper way.

Quietly, I asked, "God, who are you?" In an audible voice, I heard, "I am he; I am here." The voice was filled with so much love and power, I almost jumped in my seat, and I quickly looked around to see if anyone else in the small room had heard what I did. When no one reacted, I realized that no one else had heard this.

I did my best to compose myself as tears quietly squeezed out the sides of my eyes and my heart filled with the most overwhelming loving feeling.

Over the course of my life, there have been many interactions with God, and often there has been turmoil as I come to know his character more, while simultaneously let go of many of the teachings of my youth that put him in a specific box and colored the God I saw in life with someone else's glasses.

As my son finished his martial arts class, I practically floated to our vehicle as I contemplated what I had heard and what it did for my heart.

Love, Kate

Something that is ever so important for each person to know is that God will speak to you in an especially personal way. I cannot tell you how or when, but he will meet your heart in a way that you can understand.

I began seeking God when I was ten years old. I looked for him long and hard; my teenage years were filled with turmoil and difficulty as I endlessly looked to know him yet found only a small measure of peace by confessing my sins. I was afraid of him and experienced great confusion by what I had been taught all my life. I longed to know him personally.

At age nineteen, while visiting a little country church where the speaker invited those who wished for prayer to go to the front of the church, I responded—as I had lots of other times in my youth—but this time, the outcome was different.

As I knelt with tears soaking my one lone tissue, I heard the speaker whisper, "God is doing surgery here." For the next thirty minutes, it felt like the most beautiful liquid of love poured over my heart, and the warmest feeling I had ever known wrapped my heart in a cozy cocoon. I walked away from that place forever changed and began a journey of sweet fellowship and discovery with my heavenly Father.

When each person seeks him, he will make himself known to them. It is only in trying to force God to be in a box we might be taught he is in, that we limit his ability to connect with us. Sometimes there is so much input from well-meaning people who teach us, that we must sort through others' opinions of who God is to know who he is to us. Seeing God through someone else's lens can serve us for a season. Do not discredit someone else's perspective of God, and do not criticize them for how they see God.

If there is something in their view that can lend you peace as you seek him, let it be so. There is a season to see through someone else's eyes, and there is a time you come to when looking to God through only your own eyes will suffice. There will also be times when you cannot rely on another person to give you the answers you seek. I have found that there are times when it is just between God and me.

This does not mean that you will not see or hear things from other people that confirm what you are seeing, and someone else might say something that connects with what you are hearing. But for some reason, we human beings often look for signs to tell us we are right, and we often look out there somewhere or to another human being to give us an answer. There can be a time for that, and other times it is just between you and God.

This is part of the personal growing-up-in-God experience I have had in my life, and this lends to my ability to mentor and nurture a season in another person's walk with God, if I am willing to be used in this way.

I felt like I lost my footing temporarily, after the release of my second book. I had found my voice and began to express it after releasing the first book, but after the second book, I was tempted to go back into hiding again. I would find something inspiring, think about posting it on social media, but then think, "That person won't like this," or "They will likely be offended by that."

I had heard comments that suggested I was unkind at times, instead of thoughtful and caring, and that I shared sacred secrets not meant for the ears of others' even though I was positive I did not. This caused me to think that the things I thought were most important to me were simply an illusion and that I simply did not believe what I claimed. I decided that if I was not kind, trustworthy, and grounded, I would begin right here, right now. If these accusations were true, I would begin from that moment to be trustworthy, kind, and grounded. The places where I had stood, unaware of my arrogant confidence that I was automatically right—places that still required softening—I allowed. I realized that, if I have nothing to defend against, then there is nothing to defend against. And the more I realized there was nothing to defend, the more peaceful I became.

Realizing there are times when, despite my best intentions, others are offended by my words or actions is a sobering revelation. It increasingly teaches me that to live my best life, I must understand that many of others' responses to what I do reflect the states of their hearts and often has little to do with mine.

It also taught me that I cannot control how someone else reacts to me. Instead, I must examine my own heart and check my motives. It also highlighted the truth that everyone is in varying degrees of development in life, and when I am floundering at times and speaking words out of intense frustration, then the person next to me may feel pain because of my words when he or she might be looking for sure footing. Thus, there are times when, despite me being unaware of it, my effect on another person has the potential to affect him or her dramatically.

The last few years have been an intense journey of discovery—a journey that required digging deep to find common ground with my husband. It was the type of experience that helped me to understand that I will need to be extra careful in commenting on or passing judgment when other relationships flounder or end.

It was a most profound struggle to understand what is important in life. It was yet another time, after discussing my struggle with my husband, that we decided to choose each other again, without a promise of resolution or the outcome. It was yet again a time of agreeing to disagree in some areas.

I realized that one of the most profound areas where my husband is a gift to me is to be a mirror and to highlight the fears in the deepest recesses of my heart. For example, where I want him to tell me, "You can do it, Kate," I have realized that I can grow to provide that encouragement to myself. I am finding the value in doing an excellent job simply because it feels good to know I have done well, instead of waiting and hoping someone else will recognize my efforts.

It has been difficult for my husband to be emotionally available to me because of the painful things written on the slate of his heart in his youth. But because of this, I have chosen to seek God to fill the void I have felt, who is really the one who was intended to fill it from the beginning. I did this as opposed to continually expecting my husband to fill this void or by finding another person to fill it. If I had done that, I might not have discovered the sweet relationship with my heavenly Father, who satisfies my heart unlike any other.

I realize to a greater degree just how delighted God is with me, his beloved daughter. He has shown himself to be relentlessly kind in his caretaking of me. He has my back even in the times I cannot see it. I can almost hear him say, "Look at her. That's my girl."

This does not mean that I quit contending for a closer relationship with the best man in my life, my husband; it simply means that my heart is satisfied in drinking from the well-spring of life that flows continually between my heart and God, and each improved state of the relationship with my husband and me is an added blessing. We are both still growing and discovering new things about each other, just as we do with God.

I understand that the reason many marriages do not thrive is because of the inability for one or both people in the relationship to overcome the pain of their youths, and the habits we develop to distract ourselves from the voids we feel help us avoid facing the lack we feel.

Often, we are looking for others to convince us of our value and to distract us from the desperation we feel to have our needs met. We end up competing instead of realizing that there is enough love for everyone and that we are on the same team. When each of us has a personal relationship with God, we can come together, supporting each other out of the abundance of love flowing from each of us.

You have heard the saying that "life is what you make it" many times. It bears telling here that I have found it to be a beautiful personal truth. For many years, I struggled with what my marriage really was, compared to what I had originally envisioned. But when I finally understood that I get to decide how I respond to what I have been given and what I have chosen, even if I chose it by default, it changed my whole outlook on life.

I kept wanting the fairy tale and felt afraid that choosing my marriage by default instead of being intentional meant that I might be missing a better life somewhere else.

What life taught me instead is that, wherever I am, there is enough love to give and receive here today, instead of looking for it somewhere out there and in another person. The man I have been married to for more than twenty-seven years has the qualities and characteristics I wanted in a life partner. It is OK that I discovered this truth many miles into my relationship with him, for if this was not my life experience, there would be a different one that was just as messy.

If I had called it quits on our marriage, I believe I would have had to learn the same life lessons with the next partner farther down the road, since happiness is not found in another human being. It is found in my relationship with my loving heavenly Father. Between God and me, I learn the secrets to life and learn the lessons and experiences I came to this life to learn and have.

I still have plenty of messy moments and am reminded often that I do not have life all figured out. My relationship with my husband has its bumpy patches at times, and there are still moments when I am affected by subconscious beliefs that cause me to see my husband as the cause of my struggles. In those times, I remind myself that since I view life and others according to my personal experiences, my lens is a bit cloudy at times. I get to challenge my perspective by having another look, this time with gratitude, through eyes of unconditional and unreserved love, and I do not need to protect myself from others. Instead, I can trust myself with what I have learned and let God take care of others just as he takes care of me.

It also bears saying that there is something to be said for a man who sets out to slay dragons, one of them being to win his wife's heart. Throughout history, many stories have been told of valiant warriors who won their maidens' hearts and hands in marriage. One of the aspects of leadership I recognize and appreciate in my husband is that of his effort in winning my heart and love.

I value the incredible life lessons I have learned throughout our marriage. I would not trade them for the world. I love this life I live, and realizing I am free to choose, allows me to love this man with my whole heart.

CHAPTER 3

My Husband, the Giant

I have given them the glory that you gave me, that
they may be one as we are one—I in them and you
in me—so that they may be brought to complete
unity. Then the world will know that you sent me
and have loved them even as you have loved me.
—John 17:22–23, NIV

WHEN I MARRIED MY HUSBAND, I UNDERSTOOD THE TEACHINGS of our church to mean that since my husband was the head of the home, he was to be served and always obeyed. Thus, I began my marriage ready to serve and obey. I asked my husband about everything, including things he had no clue about since he was my provider, and I kept our home for us.

In my level of immaturity, it did not occur to me that the answers my husband gave, when I asked what to do, might have simply been an idea and not a sign that his idea was the only right way. I took his answers as the only way forward, and frustration grew because I had my own ideas of how to do things but thought I had to do them his way instead.

Today, I realize that what I brought to our marriage is a most valuable contribution and is no less important than my husband, the bread winner's contribution. I would tell younger Kate that what she does daily in laundry, cleaning, cooking, gardening, taking care of all the household chores, helping clean rental properties, and, in my case, giving birth to and mothering his children—everything she thought was her husband's—is equally hers. Without her, he would not have this family.

Today, I realize how easy this makes it for men to be inconsiderate when they do not have their ways questioned. Everyone should have his or her authority checked. Especially husbands. When a husband has a good heart, as mine did, he will be considerate of his spouse, yet he still might run over the spouse's feelings at times due to believing he is the lord of the home. This happened a lot through no fault of my husband. He simply led where I was inclined to follow, whether good or less than ideal, because I thought I had to follow him.

Please take note: a husband should be valued and respected as a leader and caretaker. I am not trying to suggest otherwise. The life of a family would be incomplete without the irreplaceable and valuable masculine protection a man brings to those he takes care of. There is a wonderful feeling of safety when a family is in the care and protection of a loving husband and father.

There is also the experience of when a husband or father dies or leaves the home, leaving a profound feeling of loss for those left behind. I am reminded of how God is to us what we need in each difficult season of life, and as incredibly painful as I am sure it is, he promises to be a husband to the widow and a father to the fatherless.

Due to misunderstandings when it comes to the value of a woman, many times, women resent men and think a man's value must be lessened and attacked to prove a woman's worth. When we recognize that men need not become less for women to be recognized as the God-designed, beautiful creatures they are, and that, without them, a man's life would be incomplete, we would understand just how much a woman's heart is worth slaying dragons for.

By understanding our personal value, we conduct ourselves with dignity and command respect from the men who would win our hearts. They will know they are winning a great treasure and that their love and respect will win a woman's allegiance, and she will happily be his partner in all the joyous moments and difficult challenges they face throughout their lives' journey together. When a woman is assured that her heart is safe in his hands, a man can trust her to put his heart in her hands too.

I found the following anonymous quote online a while back, and it reminded me of the importance of not being so wrapped up in my own needs that I forget to fill my husband's love tank too. Since I saw my husband as a giant for a lot of our marriage, it took time for me to realize the value of expressing appreciation for all he does and the effect it would have on him. When we feel like victims of life, at times we do not see the importance of giving validation to those we love. The quote I found says, "Husbands, too, deserve to be spoiled, told they are handsome, told their efforts are appreciated, and should be made to feel secure. If he is doing his best to treat you like a queen, do your best to treat him like a king. His need to feel loved and appreciated is real."

In our early years, my lack of understanding and frustration with our situation made my husband eventually feel like an immovable giant in my life. Hear me when I say that I do not mean this to sound harsh but rather simply to describe how imbalance creates a mess in the heart of the home. I kept trying to give in the way I was taught was right, but it got to the place where I thought our marriage would break me and I was unsure I could survive it.

My husband had dreams and goals to achieve in life, and I fully supported him. I had goals and dreams too, but they were so long buried that I could not remember what they were, and I did not think there was room for what I wanted.

As my frustration with stifled creativity grew, so did some faint memories of childhood dreams, though few. As a young Amish girl, I had thought I would grow up to be a wife and mother, but I had also dreamed of writing books when I grew up.

A few years into our marriage, while cleaning my kitchen, it occurred to me that I could choose to go through the cleaning process exactly as I please. That may sound funny to someone who naturally would do as they please, but for me, to be intentional with my choices was a novel idea. A variety of new awareness like this in my life helped me to let go of what I thought was the only way to live and to learn to make personal choices that set me free to bloom within our marriage as the unique individual I am.

Early on, because of how I viewed our marriage, I put my husband in the place of being unwilling to bend in many areas, and I struggled with resenting him because of it. As I grew into myself, it was a challenging experience for my husband to adapt to this evolving woman when he married a young, blindly submissive girl.

My nurturing disposition, along with the desire to please and be liked by others at any cost, made me vulnerable to struggling with finding my place, a healthy place, in my life. Because my husband was much older, I automatically thought he was the strongest, more mature, and smarter person between the two of us. The effect my life experiences had on me ensured my self-esteem hovered near the bottom of the barrel, and it was imperative that I grew to know who I was and who I was designed to be.

My husband seemed to be a giant because I saw myself as a victim. I had a problem with our relationship, and as I struggled to give what I thought was needed, we seemed to be at an impasse. Though I occasionally broached the subject of our dysfunction, he became increasingly unwilling to discuss our problems, as they seemed unfixable to him, and I grew to feel ever more hopeless. We limped along year after year, though, with some happy moments and some sad ones.

Today, I understand a woman will often feel better by discussing her frustrations and will not necessarily require things to be fixed to feel better. A man, on the other hand, wants to fix things and will feel frustrated when repeatedly discussing a subject or issue that feels impossible to resolve.

We come to this life with a desire to love and to be loved. Frequently, as we are raised by the families we are born into, there are flawed practices, and because of each person's upbringing, this affects us as children and often confirms to be true the beliefs we have within us that we are unlovable.

When our parents are not aware of just how loved they are by their heavenly Father, it is difficult for them to convey the same unconditional love to their children. Instead, they pass the fractured views of love to us, and those emotions become a part of our own belief systems.

This reminds me of the impact that my belief that I was unlovable had on our relationship, especially the early years. I desperately wanted my husband to love me even though I could not be kind to myself. If my marriage has taught me anything, it is this: being unable to be kind to myself early in our relationship determined that I could not receive acceptance from my husband.

> Dear Kate,
>
> I invite you to explore the depths of the girl's heart hidden within your chest. Ask her about the dreams of her youth. Give her a chance to play. Invite her to tell you about the long-held ideas buried beneath the responsibilities of life after you wake up one day and realize you forgot some of those dreams and that you forgot to follow those dreams with intention. Instead, you fell into line with the expectations you think others had for you.
>
> Love, Kate

I would like to tell you about the day I woke up to realize that much of what I thought others expected of me was, in fact, only the restraints I put on myself. I lived according to what I thought others wanted, and I felt resentful over those expectations. In reality, no one said many of the things I told myself.

I made an appointment with an acquaintance who was training to be a life coach. As we delved into the fears I felt, I realized I gave my husband credit for many of them; I felt he was the one who stood between me and my dreams.

As she asked me questions, one by one, those questions got closer to my heart, and as I answered them, it came down to an awareness that even if my husband did not support my dreams as I conveyed them to him, did he not support me, or was he simply trying to protect me? I came to understand that he did support me. It was simply that our lack of effective communication kept me from realizing it.

There were many times when I would cry in response to his reactions to my voicing a new idea. I wanted him to say, "You can do it; I believe in you." Since he did not realize what I wanted to hear, those words did not come. And since I did not have faith in my ability to create my dreams, everything hinged on his response.

Without my husband—the one who knows me best—reinforcing my ideas, they continually fell to pieces. If he, who knew me better than anyone else, did not believe I was capable, then surely that meant I was not good enough.

Without realizing it at times, we avoid going after the dreams in our hearts, blaming others for being in our way and making them responsible for what we do not achieve. For example, if I thought my husband was the bad guy, standing between me and what I wanted, it allowed me to escape accountability with what I do with my life. I saw it affect me the same way as my belief in who God was, where I put all responsibility on him, waiting until I got the OK to move ahead with an idea. This is not to say that there are not times when we wait for direction before we make a move, but putting everything on God can be a convenient way for us to refuse to grow in him and put off doing what we know we should.

When we know we can trust God and are open to his direction, it allows us to go about our days having full confidence in him to redirect out paths when there are better ones for us.

Answering the tough questions with my life coach opened my eyes to reality: I am the only person in my way. My husband may not support every idea I have, but if I am willing to ask different questions, I will discover ideas he does support. If his goal is to protect me, or if he feels fearful of some of the ideas his wife—who is a dreamer—has, am I going to keep looking for the path that works for us both, or am I going to allow his questions to stop me and decide for me that I simply am not allowed to dream?

Much of the way I believed was developed by the church teachings ministered to me during my youth. But since everyone hears a different version of what is taught, we often receive different answers; therefore, I may have "received" the answer I wanted at the time because it allowed me to stay in my cozy little box, where life felt safer than it would have if I had been aware that I had a choice.

Even though I grew increasingly frustrated with the way I related to my husband, it was a powerful gift. It caused me to dig for the answers to the questions in my heart until I could see, regardless of his resistance, how to live true to the dreams in my heart. With a lot of digging, we both came to an agreement on how to continue, and even though there was upheaval at first, we compromised. When I would find peace in each circumstance, my husband would find peace too.

While living in the little farmhouse perched near our semibusy road, with its old slanting floors and uneven walls, we discussed many options for a new build on the same property. My husband wanted to build behind and off to the side of the old house so we could keep it as property that we could rent out to someone else. This made sense from a financial perspective, which was important to my husband, but not from an aesthetic standpoint, which was important to me.

I looked at many options and could not get comfortable with the idea of building a beautiful new home where you had to look past an old broken one in our front yard. The first time I mentioned tearing down the old house, my husband seemed quite upset by my suggestion, stated that he thought it was a terrible idea, and promptly made an appointment to look at a home for sale across town. I was a little miffed with his reply but decided to keep looking at other options.

The fact that I kept plodding on tells you I had grown within my own skin from the quiet, timid girl he married. We could not find a property that checked off all the things he wanted, so I kept going over our options on the existing property. After my husband had a few weeks to mull over the idea of putting the old house to eternal rest, he began to talk about what the new house would look like and the best spot for its placement. Eventually, we went ahead with plans that included the removal of the old house, and today, the old, little, memory-filled farmhouse is long gone, with only pictures proving it once existed. My husband loves our property more than ever, and to hear him tell it, you would never know it was originally a point of contention between us, which fills my heart with gratitude.

This was such a powerful life lesson for me. Just because my husband did not embrace my idea to begin with, did not mean it was not a great one. Today, I do not mention our disagreement with him. I think it would be unkind, and it is not good to keep bringing up old, painful experiences or mistakes our spouses have made. I will simply tell you about it to show the power of innovative ideas and the potential for a great outcome, even when it starts with a difficult conversation, and especially when you struggle to trust your own voice.

This experience, and others like it, showed me I have great ideas and that just because others do not agree, does not mean I should discredit myself. When my husband, as part of our team of us, does not like an idea, I keep looking until I find an idea we can both agree on. I am quick to agree to any idea he has and support what he wants. I wanted him to do the same for me. Although he is generous and wants to please me, he is not so inclined. In general, I must ask for what I want.

It has been beautiful to see how this dynamic has served well in driving me to discover my own value and not being dependent on another human being's ability to see it. Instead, as I have learned to lean in while in communion with my heavenly Father, he has repeatedly coaxed me with his loving kindness and convinced me of his complete acceptance of me, quirks and all, resulting in confidence in my own abilities and thus making me a better partner for my husband.

I am a work in progress. I must still remind myself some days that it is OK to spend time on things for myself, even if someone else does not tell me I deserve it. Knowing I am loved and valued encourages me to ask for the things I want.

CHAPTER 4

In Defense of Kate

He will cover you with his feathers, and under
his wings you will find refuge; his faithfulness
will be your shield and rampart.
—Psalm 91:4

FROM AN EARLY AGE, I CAN RECALL FEELING THE NEED TO BE IN control of my surroundings to feel safe. As an adult, I could have told myself it was not possible to be in control of things entirely, and it would have served me well to be aware of this. But as with many details in life, we learn them during the journey and realize the validity in the statement that "hindsight is twenty-twenty."

As a child, the need to protect myself in this way provoked me to lie when scared. Many times, it would have made more sense to tell the truth, but fear overtook logic. Being afraid of judgement and punishment meant that I was always hypervigilant and ready to give others whatever they wanted to keep the peace. It also caused me to over give and be vulnerable to those who would abuse my willingness to please others at any cost.

This way of coping affected my approach to my husband too. In the early years of our marriage, I could not handle the least bit of criticism without breaking into tears. To me, criticism meant I was a failure.

It did not occur to me that when my husband criticized something I had done, it did not automatically mean I was wrong; it could simply mean that he disliked it. I was used to accepting others when they did something I disliked, but I could not give myself the freedom to be seen as less than perfect, which left no room for criticism. It was exhausting.

> Dear Kate,
>
> Something I have noticed over the course of my life is that we human beings have an intense desire to be understood. Frequently, when we feel misunderstood or helpless, we tend to complain or lash out at others, blaming them for our inability to deal with opposing opinions and be comfortable with who we are when others disagree.
>
> One of the secrets I have learned is that when you give up the need to be understood, it brings an incredible amount of peace into your life. When you are OK with others not understanding you, you no longer work to gain other people's approval.
>
> When you feel settled and no longer concern yourself with whether others agree with you, and it turns out they do not agree, it does not threaten your existence. You understand that you simply have a difference in opinion or do not connect with them, and that is OK. You are free to live by your convictions as you believe and so are they.
>
> Love, Kate

All my life, I have been the kind of person who loves everyone, but when I have occasionally come face-to-face with a person I just do not like, it has made me feel quite uncomfortable. I question whether there is something wrong with me because surely, it is not acceptable to dislike anyone. There might be a good reason for this sometimes. If I do not especially care for someone, and I have examined my heart and rechecked my perspective and still do not feel like my heart aligns with the person, I think this may be to help me choose what is best for myself. It does not mean that I hate this person; I simply might not feel comfortable being in a close friendship or a close relationship with them. That also does not mean the other person is evil or wrong; it seems to me that it is simply either a difference in perspective or that we are not called to walk next to them through life, but maybe just a season of life. And there is always a chance that in the future, we will connect.

Being aware of this enables me to set them free to walk their own journeys, knowing it is not up to me to decide who is right and who is wrong. God takes care of each one of us.

Dear Kate,

There will be times when you share something close to your heart, and because of how someone else feels about life, he or she will quickly stomp on what you shared. Even though your first reaction might be to stomp back, take time to consider, even though your intention might be to share something helpful. Although it might be helpful to some, depending on their life experiences, it may come across as painful to others. Give room for that.

This reminds me of the time I shared with a loved one that I had experienced anxiety for most of my childhood and experienced panic attacks as a teenager, and how, through my personal relationship with God and discovering rest in who he is for me, it completely dissolved my anxiety. The loved one reacted angrily when I shared this because, as this person put it, God has not been like that for that individual.

What was a gift to me made the person next to me angry. I meant well, but my loved one was feeling unloved and was not sure if God would do that in this person's life. What I shared did not feel helpful, even if the reason I shared my personal experience was because I wanted to give the person hope.

Do not take it personally when the reaction is angry or unkind. It is OK. At the same time, do not tiptoe around people. I understand this can be especially difficult for you because you have always wanted to please people. I have noticed, though, that you feel the need to grow in this area and are willing to be seen and to let other people hear what is in your heart. Sometimes that is a good season too.

This does not mean it will be embraced by everyone who hears it. That is OK. Let it be what it is and know that it will be good for those who want to hear what you have to say. The important thing in all this is that, if you want to share, that is good; but do not share simply because you need others to hear you to confirm your feelings or prove you are right. Know that, throughout life, there might be hundreds of times when you say something with good intentions, but the words fall flat. You will feel humbled and disappointed. That is OK too.

Do not be concerned about proving you are right. Have you not discovered through life that you have been found in error along the way at times? And did it not also turn out each time that, in altering your course, life righted itself? Choose to live in peace and love others from the abundance of God's love in your heart.

During the moments when you feel the need to be heard most, it may seem that no one hears you. When this has happened to me, it has always proven to be an area where I needed to grow in my identity with God; otherwise, I rely on others' approvals to be settled with who I am.

You can always find someone to agree with you, but sometimes it is good to sit quietly with what you believe and come to an understanding with what you are experiencing, while letting others have their space. Confirmation will come to you and let you know whether where you are is right or if there is a need for you to change something.

Love, Kate

Dear Kate,

I know what it is like to feel things deeply. At times, this makes you feel you do not belong. You will see things that you think are obvious, while others might think you a little odd for seeing what they clearly think is not there.

You as a seeker will want to discuss things you have discovered about life. At times, you might start a conversation about such things only to realize it is not necessarily a welcome subject to others. This will require wisdom. You will need to rely on intuition to know when to speak and when to remain silent.

There will be some who get you and others who think you are clearly "off the beaten path." Do not take it personally. Living true to who you are will bring the people who are interested in the same things into your life.

It can feel like you do not belong if you find that you feel differently about life than most of those around you, but be patient and keep looking; from this, you will find and connect with people you might otherwise not have met, and you will learn beautiful truths from them that will serve you for the rest of your life.

Love, Kate

A few years ago, I woke up with the realization that something I had experienced the previous night revealed that God wanted to heal my fears of being misjudged and of being afraid of what people think of me.

I had been aware since I was as young as twenty-five that I felt incredibly defensive and like it was not OK for me to make a mistake. For the first few years after my husband and I reconciled, after a period of separation in the early years of our marriage, when another person left a marriage, he would say, "They are so selfish."

This affected me deeply because I made the decision to leave our marriage at a time when I had no choice but to leave because it felt like I was drowning. At the time, I did not realize that things I had experienced as a child were having a detrimental effect on our relationship and contributing to my inability to deal with the challenges we faced.

It hurt my heart when he thought of me as selfish, when I had always lived my life to please others. Today, I realize he was speaking from a place of pain, and when I put myself in his shoes, I understood his perspective of having the woman he loved leave him and break his heart. By viewing him as a giant and myself as a mouse, I was unable to understand at the time how much my leaving affected him.

Over the years, a few instances, such as the feedback from some concerning the second book I wrote, affected me deeply because some people thought my intentions may have been to hurt them with words or that I might have been frustrated with family dynamics over the years.

As I stated earlier, one night, while feeling pained over having my motives misjudged and feeling misunderstood to an overwhelming degree, which was accompanied by an intense desire to escape this pain because I did not think I could deal with it any more intensely, I asked God to protect my heart while I let it flow through me and leave my body, since my heart physically hurt to the point where I feared I was experiencing a heart attack.

I was determined not to leave this place until I was OK with things, regardless of what others may think of me, and until I was OK with how I feel about me. After a few hours, a lot of tears, and some time spent journaling, I felt ready to resume life with a renewed sense of gratitude for who I am and a willingness to live without worrying about other people's opinions of me.

Looking back, I can see it coming to a head by my life's experiences and seeing that my children experienced some of that same defensiveness, including how it increasingly affected my relationship with my daughter the year prior. I think it has caused me to stay frozen in place with decision-making at times because I viewed making a mistake the same as being a failure.

The reoccurring emotions and accusations I had dealt with in my mind since my second book were ones that said I am not smart and that

I am simply unaware of it, and I lack common sense. Feedback from my daughter during the year 2020 and the number of times a sibling had corrected me about something I had written only heightened this fear.

At each point, it felt like my "knowing" in key moments was questionable, such that I could not trust it because when I thought I "knew" something, feedback was that some see it differently, so I must have been wrong.

You know how, when an artist draws or paints a piece of art, everyone comes to look at it and appreciates its beauty? In writing and sharing the art I created, my art hurt some of those I love most and could not be celebrated. It was the loneliest of places to find myself in. What good purpose could that have? my heart asked. I had never let myself feel the pain of the rejection of something I had created until that night. Through feedback from the written art I had created, I finally realized that what was life-giving to some was pain-giving to others who matter most to me.

This journey with Jesus is not about perfection and is not one without mistakes. Our imperfection teaches us in the learning process. Coming to grips with my imperfections in this experience taught me that it was OK to have flaws, and the world would not fall apart if I simply apologized for causing unintentional pain to others.

Since my book had been a blessing to some and brought hurt to others, I came to realize that I could not control how others perceived me or experienced me. I had to let go of control in this area. In listening to someone share a message, five people can hear something entirely different. We all have a different view on life since our experiences are unique to us.

Dear Kate,
Choose to live with an open heart. Do not spend your time defending what you believe. If what you believe is true, it will stand. It is not your responsibility to convince others that you are right.

Love, Kate

CHAPTER 5

My Brother's Keeper

I find it beautiful when someone prays for you
without you knowing. I do not think there
is any form of deeper or purer love.
—Unknown

I REMEMBER THE DAY I BECAME AWARE THAT I HAD POSITIONED myself within our relationship as someone meant to save my husband because he had experienced separation from his father and his family. I thought that since he was estranged from his family, that meant I needed to fill the gap and take care of him in God's stead.

I would never have expected him to do that for me, and when I realized that I was trying to save him, I felt surprised and humbled at my perceived self-importance. I proposed in my heart to let him take care of himself, while simply loving him and giving him room to figure out his own path. I realized he was no longer a young boy but a man who was capable of being who he was without me catering to the little boy in him. It is probable that I was affecting his personal development by mothering him in areas not designed for me to do so, actively putting myself in God's place, and creating frustration within our relationship.

It is also probable that the root of this behavior stems from the belief that when we experience salvation according to our understanding of the

Bible and must go out and save the world, without realizing it, we place ourselves in the position of Savior in others' lives, even for our loved ones.

We forget that God sends his word to each person. I am reminded of the verse in Romans 14:11 (NIV). It is written, "As surely as I live says the Lord, every knee will bow before me, every tongue will acknowledge God." It is good for others to see that we have a good Father. It is also good for God to be delighted to be seen with us because we are a good example of his love, and because when we allow him to support us, when others see how we live, they will want to know him too.

When we talk to others out of the desire to save them, as opposed to simply being motivated to share from the abundance of love and the goodness of God and the incredible life he supports us with, it often leaves strangers feeling like we only share about salvation to relieve our consciences. When we cannot help but bubble over with the joy we experience from God's love, it is inevitable that others will want to know him too. To win someone over out of obligation might be honorable, but to win them out of the abundance of God's love in our heart is wonderful.

A few years ago, I said to a friend, "I sure would hate to be a Pharaoh in someone's life." The thought that followed at once was, *Wait, what if I had been a Pharaoh?* The next thought was, *It is likely that I have been a Pharaoh in someone else's life.*

If you will remember, Pharaoh was the ruler in the story from the Bible about the children of Israel who were enslaved in Egypt and who worked to earn their freedom for many long years, yet Pharaoh would repeatedly find a reason to delay their freedom, continuing to build his own kingdom with the labor of his slaves. I read all about this story in the Bible, in the book of Exodus.

It is not that I intentionally create obstacles for others as Pharaoh did, but I refer to it because, depending on how others are affected by me, they may view me as the enemy of their freedom in the same way I have thought that others who have brought me pain, stood between me and my freedom.

I might be standing in a place where another person struggles to deal with something I have said or done, even if my intentions were not meant to cause pain; it may take just as much effort on their part to heal as it has for me. This is a humbling realization to come to and reminds me anew to taste my words before they leave my mouth, yet at the same time, to live openly and honestly, knowing I cannot live carefully enough to guarantee I will not hurt another person by being who I am. If I allow this and walk where I am called, what someone else views as an obstacle might be the very opportunity for a lie they are believing about themselves to be uncovered. I have come to know this has worked for me in my own life.

What if experiencing or viewing me as a Pharaoh for a time eventually reveals to that person a new perspective that previously held a blind spot for them and now becomes a gift in his or her life? What if I let others experience me as they will and realize that, though it may make me feel sad if others misunderstand me, if I am not concerned with how they experience me, what if it is a gift to them and a part of their journeys to freedom? How about I just live?

Our parents, families, and the friends we do life with give us many opportunities to learn. Some of the experiences are incredibly painful for a season but end up bearing beautiful fruit in our lives. Since many interactions with those we love can be unclear because of our perspectives, choose to see the person's heart, even if it is yet unhealed. Give grace to yourself and to those you love as you both chart unfamiliar territory. By taking time to heal the different areas of our hearts, in what seems like trivial details but that affect our daily lives, our hearts can become softer, less guarded, and expand to receive God's love and acceptance in a greater measure.

> Dear Kate,
>
> Place your heart in a position to partner with God and to heal. We can go kicking and screaming through life, resisting our hearts being saturated with God's love in deeper ways, or we can choose to grow up in him and walk with boldness, allowing ourselves to be seen by others as they will, being a vessel through which others might experience new freedoms, just as we do by the examples of other who live with open and joyful hearts.
>
> Love, Kate

Dear Kate,

It is good to stand up for yourself. It is exceedingly difficult when you have not stood up for yourself in the past. Just remember, no, you cannot control whether others feel hurt by you standing up; however, if in standing up for yourself, you blame someone else for why you could not do so before, it will bring pain to that person because you are making him or her responsible for your inability to stand on your own. The things you say will be loaded with emotion, and the other person will feel the pain from your judgment and you will not experience the outcome you are hoping for.

When it comes to your parents, do not be so close-minded that you refuse the wisdom they have developed with age, just because you might disagree with them on key points. The vigor of youth is ever so valuable, but so is the wisdom of age. Give credit to your parents for the things they have learned and even though you may speak a different language than they do at times, do not discredit how much they can contribute to your life.

Remember, when you respond to them as though they do not know anything, it creates challenges within your relationship, and it is obvious that you lack wisdom. Do not be sarcastic and discredit the advice they give you. You may wholeheartedly disagree, and that is OK, but receive their wisdom and their advice with respect and gratitude when they show that they care and want to be a part of your life.

Love, Kate

Many parents and children who are unable to have a relationship wish they had one with each other. Some do not have the opportunity due to one of the family members having passed on, or because of one family member's choice to disengage from his or her life. If you have a parent who is plugged in, even when you get annoyed, take time to feel gratitude.

Those who do not have a parent mourn their loss. Those who have parents and do not have a good relationship with them mourn the awareness of what they could have. Those whose parents or children live in dysfunction—whether it be with the obvious, such as drugs and alcohol, or other, not-so-obvious coping mechanisms—mourn for what could be.

In whatever state you and your family find yourselves, feel gratitude for what is good and pray for what you would change. Deuteronomy 5:16 (NIV) says, "Honor your father and mother, as the Lord your God has commanded you, so that you may live long and that it may go well with you in the land the Lord your God is giving you" and has a deeper meaning for me than just doing what my parents want and following their examples as I was taught in my youth.

Many times, as we grow up, we see things differently than our parents do; we believe differently, and we often live in defense of our new beliefs or thoughts or ideas. When we make decisions in defense of something or in resistance to someone, we are not choosing something; instead, we are reacting to something by default. Making peace with where we are and the houses that built us gives us the freedom to make healthy life decisions.

Colossians 3:23–24 (NIV) says, "Whatever you do, work at it with all your heart, as if you are working for the Lord, not for human masters, since you know that you will receive an inheritance from the Lord as a reward. It is the Lord Jesus Christ you are serving." I find this verse to be a beautiful reminder not to choose honoring your parents and others only when you feel they deserve it but rather because it reflects your personal values, and how you treat others reflects more on who you are than it does on the behavior of others.

When you live in reaction to what you have been taught, it might cause you to make choices that are negative for yourself or to discredit your parents or elders or disrespect them, but more than hurting them, you hurt yourself. Until we heal what drove us away from our raising, we are not able to see the beauty in what may have been the very reason we were born into the families God placed us in.

Today, I also notice that sometimes, we as parents can be defensive when our children talk about the pain they experienced as children.

I have been a child, and I have been a parent. Both have their painful seasons and times. I think, as parents, we must be patient and not automatically take our children speaking up about their pain as a disrespect to us. It can prove challenging to hear about the pain we might have caused them, especially when we come from families or cultures that do not typically express their emotions, and it might feel like completely unfamiliar territory. I understand that it is painful for us because we love our children, want the best for them, and hope we have done an excellent job raising them.

Some children will love us unconditionally and forgive us for our mistakes, and others, it feels, will stick it to us and tell us where we went wrong and repeatedly rehash hurtful experiences, expecting that if we will just understand how much pain we caused them, we will apologize efficiently and things will finally be healed.

Although this is painful, each experience brings grace to our hearts. I often hear people say they want to know God's heart and be as he is. I think with any pain we feel coming from our children, God would have to feel coming from us through the many seasons of our lives, especially when we mistake what he allows in his wisdom with what we think he should protect us from by his love.

> Dear Kate,
>
> It is vitally important to check your perspective. When you feel intense pain, it is easy to see life and everybody in it through that lens and to be convinced that your perspective is correct. When you are looking through the eyes of trauma, your views will be askew.
>
> Love, Kate

Young people often want their parents to accept their latest ideas and perspectives and sometimes lash out at their parents if this is not the case, demanding tolerance from their parents but lacking it themselves when their parents do not readily embrace their new views.

As parents, when everything is flowing along smoothly, it is easy for us to take credit for how well our children have turned out, and it is just as easy to condemn ourselves as failures when our children are not doing well in life, even if just for a season.

Being aware of this helps me to simply feel gratitude when my children are doing well, and although I am humbled and imperfect in remembering, when they are experiencing a season or many seasons of struggles, I am increasingly reminded not to get swept up in the turmoil they are feeling but to pray from a place of peace and agreement with God for the outcome he wants for them, which is always for their best, despite the sometimes bumpy and crooked paths of the journey.

As I mentioned, I have been a child, and I have been a parent. To love my children and have them tell me where I went wrong, did wrong, and how much I hurt them, is, in some ways, even more painful than the pain I experienced as a child. It is humbling and hurtful, and it also shows us how, in many areas of life, we come full circle and learn what it means to experience the challenges of each season.

Sitting while you are being told just how much damage your words or actions caused your child, the tears that eventually refuse to be restrained will wash your face, as you wait, without defense, while words fail you and the onslaught from your children rends your heart in two. You may wonder how it is that this child who adored you through his or her childhood has suddenly turned on you, shredding the hope you had that you had parented well, even a little.

Hear me when I say that it does not occur to this child you raised that his or her words can bring indescribable pain to you; for you, the parent, are a giant in their eyes. They grow to match your physical size, yet within them still beats a child's heart, vulnerable to you in a way unlike anyone else.

Trying to express your intentions would be moot; their pain is too great. Through it all, have the courage to listen and wait. Acknowledge their feelings and let them know you hear them. When you owe them an apology, apologize. If you do not remember, it is OK to say so, and at the same time, express your perspective and or intentions. Be mindful not to discredit their pain just because you might not remember, though.

If they continue to rehash these experiences over time, even after you hear, listen, and apologize to them, it is OK to ask them to stop. The boundaries they are learning go both ways. It might take many years for them to realize that you could not apologize proficiently enough to heal them. Healing will come to their hearts through their personal relationships with God.

It is also important not to parent them out of guilt, though there are many instances that have supplied the opportunity to feel guilty. One of my friends shared this with me many years ago, and it has lent wisdom to my parenting experience and enabled me to check my responses along the way in each interaction with my children.

When you respond to your children out of guilt, you are unable to make the best decisions for them, and some children will notice your guilt and use it against you. If you are like me, you experience guilt in plenty of areas, and you feel you could have parented better.

It is likely that not every parent will have this experience because some families are not open to this level of intense dialogue, or their children might not feel free to express themselves in this way. To have this experience is a bittersweet gift. Painful though it is, the levels of understanding for both parties are potentially life-changing and might eventually enable your children to be more effective parents, should they have children of their own.

Sometimes, by having intense conversations, the children will suddenly see their parents through new eyes. They will realize their parents are no giants but human beings with painful things written on the slate of their hearts, too, and are learning what it is to be a parent right along with their children. Many times, by being willing to have difficult conversations, it brings us to a new level of understanding with each other and encourages forgiveness for both parents and children.

Most of us experience each age of the human being's existence through life on earth. When someone we love dies young, we often see them through our eyes without judgment, remembering only the good parts for the rest of our lives. Those who stay, love us, although imperfectly, and we experience all the flaws and human relationship struggles that we do not get to experience with the person who passed away.

> Dear Kate,
>   As we go through life, we often want to be right, and we want what we believe to be right because it

makes us feel safe. Our perspectives can always be challenged, and sometimes it is healthy for us to have our views challenged. In each instance where your perspective is challenged, take time to reflect on it. Be open to instruction and critique when given, even when delivered in a negative manner. Do not be so defensive that you cannot receive instruction. Be teachable. Be curious. Be open. Be loving.

Know you will see things differently when you are forty than you did at twenty, and no doubt, you will see things differently when you are sixty than you did at thirty.

Always be open and kind, but do not be so kind as to let it overwhelm wisdom. Yes, stand up for yourself, but make sure that when you are standing up for yourself, you are not defensively blaming your parents or others for your problems.

I have often heard it said that, "You cannot help what happened to you as a child, but it is up to you who you are after you become an adult." As an adult, when you blame someone else for your problems or for being your obstacle, you are crippling yourself from being able to learn and grow freely and to experience a life you find joy in.

Love, Kate

CHAPTER 6

Visible and Transparent

Therefore, confess your sins to each other and pray
for each other so that you may be healed. The prayer
of a righteous person is powerful and effective.
—James 5:16, NIV

Dear Kate,

Are you willing to be seen and heard as you are?
Are you willing to share the wisdom you have garnered
thus far in your life? Are you willing to deal with the
extraordinarily strong opinions of some and give them
room to have their opinions and still have your own, if
you feel comfortable in them? Are you willing to author
a book and take the time to really know you have given
it your best, give it to a publisher, and let them market
it and allow it to do what it will?

Love, Kate

AT TIMES, I FIND IT INCREDIBLY CHALLENGING WHEN PEOPLE
have strong opinions in areas I believe differently, just be at
peace with the tension in a moment or a season of turmoil.

Can I allow room for my opinion and someone else's point of view too? I am still learning.

Hiding is one of the things I did well for most of my life. I wanted to feel known and seen, but I felt intensely uncomfortable with being the center of attention—so much so that, when it happened, my face would turn a bright shade of red. The desire to hide was accompanied by the fear of intimacy, the kind of intimacy that would result in others not liking me if they really knew the innermost parts of me. This was, of course, a lie, but it appeared true to me.

Hiding worked well for me for quite a while, but gradually, I realized I did not come to this life to hide but rather to live graciously, boldly, confidently, and transparently. To truly live means I must be willing to be visible. Being visible will result in some people expressing a distaste for me. To be OK with this has been one of the most challenging life lessons to date, yet I have come to appreciate it immensely.

The person closest to my heart, requiring the most vulnerability, my husband, gives me a lot of practice and is the most important relationship for me to be visible in. Since I have committed to sharing my life with him, I want to invest effort into having a great relationship with him just as I would in building any other life skill. Thus, I am confronted often with areas I have not practiced being seen.

Through experiences as a child, I learned to rely on myself and not to ask others for help. I applaud the young me for being resilient and for taking care of herself to the best of her ability, but the time came when it was important for her to learn to ask for help from others and to realize she does not have to go through life alone.

There are times throughout our marriage relationships when we feel hurt or offended by something our spouses say, and frequently, upon reflection, we come to realize the reason we feel hurt or offended is because of the glasses through which we view ourselves. In being willing to check our perspectives, we find it easier to overcome an offense or not to be offended in the first place.

There are also times when it takes a bit longer than others to work through the emotions these offenses bring and to keep our hearts open. Being willing to examine our responses and by allowing ourselves to be soft at times and ask for support when we need it helps us to be resilient in a new and more effective way. To say putting this into practice has been difficult for me, seems like an understatement. The first few times I asked for support from my husband, things did not go well. This is not surprising, given my tendency to be independent, take care of myself, and not to trust anyone on an emotional level. His response did not encourage me to ask for support, but the gift was, as I tried a few more times, he gradually adjusted to the new, softer side of me and began to show support when I needed it.

This taught me the value of showing up differently and the wisdom in the statement, "We teach others how to treat us." Many times, we simply do not know how to conduct ourselves to receive the responses we want. Instead, through trauma, we learned to ask for it in ineffective ways, and our reception is a bit prickly, which does not encourage those who love us to get intimately close.

In fact, I am still learning to be OK with knowing that when someone else is displeased with me, life still goes on and although another person might not always like how I am, since I am OK with others being imperfect and unlikable sometimes, I am increasingly at peace with me being found unlikable at times too.

The area I have been educated in recently is speaking up when something does not feel right to me, especially when others intently disagree. To deal with discourse with the person directly involved is incredibly difficult at times and requires a lot of courage. As a rule, family members and friends talk to each other about a problem with others instead of with the one the problem concerns. This enables us to avoid confrontation and remain invisible when it is healthier to be seen.

Frequently, we are hurt by something a loved one does or says, and our minds can run away with negative assumptions. Many times, if we talk to the person involved, it alleviates much of the misunderstanding because we get to hear the intentions of the person's heart even if the delivery was imperfect.

During the times we do disagree, it is a good exercise in practicing unconditional love. When we see others doing something we believe is wrong or harmful, it can evoke strong feelings of discomfort. This is often when we discuss these wrongs with others instead of leaving things alone for the individual to figure out. When we really care for someone's well-being, we can pray for and bless him or her without pointing out the person's wrongs to someone else.

Many times, in examining our own hearts, we will notice our intentions are to discuss the other person's wrongs because that makes us feel better about our own wrongs or makes us be glad that at least we know better and would never make the choices this other person does. I think this stems from the belief that we are unlovable and not enough, thus, by comparing ourselves and seeing that we are doing things better, we can feel good about ourselves—at least in that one area.

By practicing being direct with those we love, we gain their confidence, and they know they can trust and count on us to be honest with them when they ask for our opinion in any given situation, even when it is incredibly difficult, and that will prove a valuable gift to them.

It takes courage and humility to speak up when we see something is wrong. At the same time, it requires just as much courage and humility to deal with the responses that our direct conversations evoke. It will not always be easy or pleasant. In another person's response, we get the opportunity to examine our perspectives and confirm they are correct, or we discover that we do not see the whole picture and that there are blind spots that our eyes are suddenly opened to. Either way, we learn something valuable through interaction.

Dear Kate,

This also brings up the importance of being approachable when someone speaks up about something you have said or done that they feel is wrong. Even when it evokes pain, it is important for you to recognize and appreciate the courage it takes for a person who values you enough to speak directly to you. I understand that many times, this is easier said than done. It is even more difficult to have a perceived wrong pointed out to you when you do not see it as wrong. Even in this, be gentle and kind. Be slow to react and take time to hear the person's concerns.

Love, Kate

Over the past few years, I have done a lot of reading, and this has resulted in my discovery of truths concerning the history of our nation that I had previously thought others were "off the beaten path" for believing as they did when they suggested everything is not as we were taught in school.

In sharing these discoveries with my husband, after responding quite animatedly and after calming down from his shock, he sweetly and gently told me that he thinks I am a bit of a conspiracy theorist. For a girl who thrived on blending in all her life, this was an intense growing experience for me. I felt angry that he refused to even look at what I had read and thought me so flaky as to arrive at a new perspective on a whim. I felt defensive that he thought of me as "one of those people," knowing that I, his wife of quite a few years, had put a lot of time and effort into educating myself, which resulted in coming to accept these truths. I was upset that he was unwilling to value my opinion more than to write me off at once. Upon reflection, I recognized he simply was not in a place where he was willing to examine what I found, for reasons that might be known only to him. I must be OK with that, just as I must be visible and true to who I am.

I was willing to broach the subject of how important it was to me that he valued what I think and showed kindness by listening without judgment, in the same way that I support his way of going through life and staying in his lane. In times like these, we do not necessarily come to an agreement, but at least by expressing our thoughts, we understand where the other is coming from and it alleviates resentment.

I must also accept him right where he is, even when we see things differently. It has proven to be another area where I am learning the value of showing up for myself while giving space for differing beliefs, even if—and especially when—it includes my spouse. To put it simply, where we see differently, we agree to disagree, which is an important habit to practice within a close relationship.

My eyes opened to a new level of understanding about why the desire to hide is so tempting. It is a rude awakening when someone abruptly disagrees with the person who lives to please people, but it also highlights why it is increasingly important for the people-pleaser to be seen as he or she is. Others learn from us when we allow ourselves to be transparent, just as we learn from them.

One of the reasons practicing visibility is imperative for me is because it keeps challenging my deeply ingrained and harmful belief in my need for perfection. Practicing continued visibility gives me the opportunity to make mistakes or to be wrong about something, and each time, I am reminded that mistakes are normal and that the outcome is personal growth. I get to know myself better and, most importantly, the world will remain standing, despite a practicing perfectionist's tendency to think it will implode.

This also creates a willingness in me to stand up for what I believe even when others tell me I am wrong. I know my heart looks for truth, and I have full confidence in God to bring me around in the areas I see incorrectly or unclearly.

It reminds me of the time a friend gave me a book, many years ago, and after leafing through it a bit, I placed it on my bookshelf where it stayed for the next six months. Leading up to this, through conversations with my friend, I learned that we differed in some beliefs, and thus, I did not think I would be interested in a book she liked. But after the six months had passed, I randomly remembered the book, opened it, and began to devour the contents. It was the right time for me to have the book in my hands. If my friend had been too afraid or unsure of my opinion, she may not have chosen to give me the book, and not planted a seed that served me well down the road.

Dear Kate,

Never underestimate the value of planting a seed, and do not be fearful of other people's responses. When you are inspired to plant a seed and willing to let the seed be received as it will, water will be poured on it at the right time, and the seed will bear beautiful fruit.

Thus, you are not hiding an important gift of love from the person walking next to you.

Have you considered the gift it is when others are vulnerable and willing to learn on a public platform? Think about the times you have seen others making a mistake or speaking wrongly and about how that opened your eyes to deal more effectively with situations that arise in your relationships. Let this inspire your willingness to be visible.

Love, Kate

CHAPTER 7

Love Is Not Heavy

Soften your forehead, unclench your jaw,
relax your shoulders. This is a reminder to
stop holding tension in your body.
—Unknown

WE LOVE HARD AT TIMES. WHEN WE SEE A NEW TRUTH, WE want everyone else to see it too. I have learned over the past few years, on occasion when I would share something, that I was sure the recipient's eyes would be opened if they just heard this truth. But there were times they did not see what I shared as truth, and instead, they saw and experienced it as a personal attack on them. They had a completely unique perspective, and although they were hearing about something I found empowering, they heard it as a threat to their existence. My disagreement with their views of someone they embraced as right or good left them feeling fearful.

This experience reminded me of all my familial relationships, past and present, and of how we love each other by the examples we are raised with. At times, we take personal responsibility for each other's lives and well-being in a way that weighs us down and makes us feel responsible for those we love.

It is our gift to realize that we are here to love and support those we love, and at the same time, set them free to live as they choose while also learning to live as we choose, each one of us loving the other with hands open and palms up. When we take responsibility for each other's lives, we tend to believe we have the right to comment on each other's choices.

Recently, I had an experience that opened my understanding in this area. After a year of intense dialogue with a loved one, I discovered something I felt could help the individual, but the person blatantly refused my offer. I felt quite frustrated that I had the potential answer, and this person was not even open to trying what I suggested, especially considering the great amount of emotional and physical energy I had invested in this.

On top of the person's refusal, my husband chimed in, agreeing with said loved one. It was a bit too much for me to deal with, having my husband side with someone else when I alone had invested all that energy. I expressed my displeasure with his input and went into my closet, closing the door behind me as I always did when experiencing the process of intense emotions, to ensure no one would see me fall apart.

I asked God to protect my heart since it felt as though I might have a heart attack yet again, and as wave after wave of "I am not enough" and the pain of rejected love rose within my chest, ragged breaths escaped, and tears dripped down my face. I clung to the shelf above me, waiting for the storm to pass, and with each new breath, I surrendered the need to be enough and to be too much.

As my breathing returned to normal, I became aware of just how much the way I understood loving someone was attached to my self-worth. Being the oldest girl in a family of nine children meant I was used to being a nurturing person, and I fulfilled this way of being by taking care of everyone else. I eventually came to realize that my desire to help, in the way I tried it, left me feeling exhausted.

When I returned to the living room with slightly red-rimmed eyes, my husband asked, as he always does, "Were you crying?"

I replied, as I always do, "No, I never cry." Then I apologized for snapping at him and explained what I had just experienced.

"Kate, you are not responsible for others," he proclaimed emphatically.

This was only one of many times that my sweet husband reminded me of this truth, but it took until this year for it to truly sink in. Ah, the growing pains of life. How blessed am I for being married to this wise man.

Over the years, when disagreements arose within my family, I made it my mission to fix things. I had gradually been coming into the awareness that, although I may have loved my family by fixing things and it highlighted the gift I have to bring peace into stressful situations and mediate tense moments, it was not how I was designed to live within my family dynamic in the long-term.

It was imperative for me to realize that my family members were each capable of conducting their own lives without my intervention, and that had increasingly blown up in my face over the years. I am a bit of a slow learner at times, and I can smile at this because I am learning to let go and be OK with the realization that I am perfectly imperfect.

Though it felt like I had to fill it for many years of my life, no one asked me to fill this space. I learned this behavior by responding to situations in the only way I knew how. By my way of loving, no doubt at times I hampered the life experiences of those I loved. It was a gift to me and to them to let go and just be me, their sibling.

Dear Kate,

Something that may be difficult to experience throughout different seasons in your life is the little-known truth that the people in your life who cause you the most pain may be the most important people you will ever know because of the important life lessons they enable you to learn.

In those times, when another person does or says something that causes you pain and it is the kind of pain that temporarily robs you of your breath, your appetite, and your sleep, take time to consider objectively what is going on in your heart, your perspective about life, and what has happened so far.

It is important to note that childhood traumas often paint our lives' perspectives, and we react to experiences in life and to other people because of the pain of that trauma.

So far, each time I have experienced this, it turns out that in taking time to sit through the pain and examine my perspectives, I have found that it has changed how I approach life, made my heart softer, more pliable, expanded it to make room for more of God's love, and helped me to understand others more effectively.

Love, Kate

Much is said these days about boundaries. Many of us were not taught what having healthy boundaries looks like growing up; instead, we learned that love is heavy and that we must save each other. This might be the result of being taught that because God saved us, we are responsible for saving others; thus, we lead in relationships and friendships with the intent to tell others the truth as opposed to giving them the freedom to come to God as he leads and draws them.

I remember hearing a line in a movie where an old prophet told a young man, "Every man's way to God is different. I hope yours is not too hard." This statement combined with my own relationship with the God I feared to approach in my youth but who, over time, I realized was actually the kindest, most optimistic, and heart-winning Father I could ever have imagined knowing, caused me to take a step back and to let go of my need to save others.

I contemplated my own experience as a teenager who sought after God with my whole heart. When the time was right, I heard the answer to my soul's cry, and God made himself known to me in beautiful ways that have surprised and delighted me at every turn.

At the same time, when, out of the abundance of our hearts, we share the love we are experiencing with God, it reaches the ears ready to hear, and there is no heaviness attached to it. It is perceived as a most-precious gift that changes our lives' experience for the better in every area.

Just as it is great to share what excites us about God, it is also important to tread gently in the lives of others. I have seen Christians trampling the boundaries of others without regard for others' experiences at times, simply because we claim to have the truth on our side. Sometimes we claim and recite freedom verses from the Bible because of what we say we believe, but the fruit of our lives does not prove that to be true. This is not to condemn us; it is an admonishment to evaluate, as a self-proclaimed child of the king, the words we speak, and to check that our actions align with what we preach, lest we leave a sour taste in the mouth of the person who does not believe in God or who no longer believes because of having been hurt by the actions of someone in the church.

Boundaries are essential. My experience with some people setting boundaries with me sometimes means they let me know where their boundaries are, but they do not always honor me by giving me the same courtesy in return. They might also be affected by how they were raised, and may I graciously allow them the space they need to learn too. Because this has happened repeatedly, I expect that this is an area I might receive help from learning more about. It is this very thing that caused me to be more aware of the importance of our actions and beliefs backing up our words and the fruit our lives produce.

In considering this valuable truth, I thought about how we do not just walk into another person's house without knocking, and even then, we do not waltz in without an invitation. In the same manner, it is good to ask permission to share something with another person, especially a stranger.

I have noticed, when I am open to listening and learning, that there are things I do not know about myself or that I am simply unaware of that potentially affect others in a negative way. By being open, I see those things and do my best to change my habits. As a result, the affect I have on those I love is from the abundance of God's love in my heart, instead of affecting them out of the fear and judgment I might be feeling.

In this way, I can show by my words and actions that love is not heavy and therefore release what is not mine to carry. I have begun to practice saying aloud often, "I release everything that is not mine to carry." This also helps me let go of things when I am unsure whether they are mine or not. This has evolved into a truth that serves me well in my relationship with my husband. It has helped me to understand there is room for both of us to learn and grow from where we are without demanding more than each can give.

Dear Kate,

You know how desperately you have wanted your husband to tell you that you are enough. Do you realize that is not his job?

You came to this life to learn that you are enough and that when your heavenly Father created you, the work of his hand, he said it was good. The Bible says, "I praise you because I am fearfully and wonderfully made; your works are wonderful; I know that full well" (Psalm 139:14, NIV). Allow this truth to take anchor in your heart and mind.

I understand that you have found life incredibly challenging at times and there have been moments you have found it difficult to believe what he said is true; I ask you to give God the time and chance to convince you of this. For the friend who is like you, do you tell him or her that he or she is not good enough? Or do you, in fact, encourage the person, tell the individual he or she is enough, and remind him or her of the beautiful and precious child God sees?

You know how you appreciate when others share their hearts, and the little bits they share enlighten your own heart and it helps you understand something that was confusing before? If you are willing to share what you have learned, it will have the same effect on someone else, and that person will appreciate hearing what is on your heart.

It is not your job to rescue others. You have carried the weight of the world on your shoulders by making that your personal responsibility. God's yoke is not heavy, and it is good to let God take care of others. It is his specialty. Your part in life is to love others as he loves you.

Love, Kate

"Let no debt remain outstanding, except
the continuing debt to love one another, for
whoever loves others has fulfilled the law"
(Romans 13:8, NIV).

CHAPTER 8

Wisdom and Compassion

Blessed is the one who finds wisdom, and the one who gets understanding, for the gain from her is better than gain from silver and her profit better than gold. She is more precious than jewels, and nothing you desire can compare with her. Long life is in her right hand; in her left hand are riches and honor. Her ways are ways of pleasantness, and all her paths are peace. She is a tree of life to those who lay hold of her; those who hold her fast are called blessed.
—Proverbs 3: 13–18, NIV

Dear Kate,

It is good to have compassion for others, but please do not pity them. This lessens the value of the challenges they have endured and the courage they have shown in overcoming each obstacle they have faced throughout their lives. Love, support, and pray for them, but do not pity them.

Each of us does what we know, even when it does not work, until we know better. And even then, at times, we stay in that place of knowing better but being unable to put into practice that which would give us a different outcome, many times because we do not realize how much God loves us. Each person will learn at his or her own pace. If you feel inspired to share something, do so knowing that some will understand and some will hear, but others will disagree. It does not make them your enemies.

You will rarely find someone who agrees with you on every single point of view. That is the beauty of everyone's journey in life. When you meet someone who agrees with you, find joy in it. If you find someone who disagrees with you, find joy in it, and reexamine your perspective. If your perspective is correct, there is no harm and no danger in examining it. If your perspective is flawed, it being challenged gives you the opportunity to see things differently, and since we humans tend to be predisposed to living in boxes where we are comfortable, these experiences present us with opportunities for our hearts to expand when it is good for us to grow and change.

Love, Kate

SOME OF US ARE SEEKERS WHO STEP OUTSIDE THE BOX BECAUSE WE are curious and want to know what new things there are to discover. We feel this gnawing curiosity to have questions answered and are dissatisfied with leaving new paths uncharted. Sometimes this causes a major disruption with our families and friends; the boxes we were born into fray at the edges and eventually break open.

Although this will often cause an incredible amount of pain for the people in our boxes, sometimes, it is necessary. This is OK.

There are others who prefer to stay in their boxes and do not care to see what is outside. They feel safe inside the boxes they have built or that someone else has built for them. This is OK too. There is room for both of us.

Discovering this truth has had a wonderful effect on me and has changed the way I view the world and people around me.

I have spent a lot of time and years being overwhelmed by the compassion I feel for others when they are experiencing pain or struggles because of—from my perspective—their harmful beliefs.

Though it is imperative to speak up if we see someone being harmed by abuse, in other areas, I have noticed that when a person wants to be free, nothing, regardless of the obstacles they must overcome, can keep them from finding their paths to freedom.

Within the dynamics of my marriage, during the season when I thought I must save my husband because he left the box of his youth and experienced the tearing away of what was familiar, I gave him a free pass for things that were not necessarily wise and that did not actually help him. When I saw him as the individual whose heavenly Father would take care of him just as he takes care of me, it enabled me to see my husband as a man who, while walking next to me through life, also has much to contribute to my life. When we both see this, it ensures that neither of us are trying to save the other; instead, we support each other as we discover new and unfamiliar territory together.

With this knowledge came a willingness to allow room for the baggage we both brought into our relationship. I realized that I could allow the messiness and still know there is enough love for everything we need, which gives me freedom to allow him the space he needs to experience restoration in the areas that were broken while living in the box of his youth and in the breaking of and leaving that box.

I am assured by my observations that it is a healthy thing to view my husband as capable of charting his own journey. It also highlights the importance of recognizing this same thing in my son, who grew from a little boy into man. By being aware of this, I support them both but am not overwhelming them with my desire to rescue and mother them.

Compassion certainly has its place, but so does wisdom. Wisdom trusts others' journeys with God as what is best for them, as opposed to what misguided compassion believes is best.

There are times when we are overwhelmed by compassion and the need to rescue, and we hamper the masculinity of the men in our lives, affecting their abilities to figure out their unique lives' paths. Instead of entrusting their journeys to God, we carry them emotionally, adding more weight to our already full plates, and when they do not respond favorably to our "love," we are disappointed and hurt because they refuse our attempts to help or rescue them.

It is incredibly important in this season for women to embrace God's design of what it means to be woman, a feminine being who is not less because of how she is designed and who does not compete with men to do what he can, but who is beautifully designed to be everything a man cannot be. By embracing all that we are, we inspire the divine masculinity of the men in our lives, as designed by God, to step up and lead from a healthy place. I recently found a quote that said, "Femininity inspires masculinity," and that resonates beautifully true to me.

A marriage will be most successful when there is a healthy balance of the masculine and feminine, each of us aware that we bring qualities and characteristics into the relationship that the other does not have. When in balance, we meet each other's needs in a beautiful way where we do not compete, but can simply be who we are and face the world together as a unified team.

Many of us women, from the traumas we experienced as children, live in defense of our lives' experiences. We see the men or parents in our lives as giants, not realizing that they, too, are products of their upbringings and are, at times, still affected by the boxes they grew up in.

> Dear Kate,
>
> You might not realize this, but by allowing God to heal the trauma-filled places in your heart, you will be able to contribute to the healthy picture of what divinely designed femininity looks like and potentially contribute to the lives of younger women and those you meet on your life's journey.
>
> Love, Kate

There is an unpleasant feeling that goes with her words when a woman who is filled with cynicism and bitterness speaks. Often, when we are in a bitter place, we say things not realizing they cut deep into those who are within hearing distance. I do not say this to criticize but simply to exhort us women into discovering who we are and living from a healthy identity in God's love.

I am sure you have heard the Bible verse, "The tongue has the power of life and death, and those who love it will eat its fruit" (Proverbs 18:21, NIV).

It is why we should be mindful that even if we do not view ourselves as people of impact, we do affect others more than we expect.

When we are rooted in a bitter place, we will not be aware of the weight of our words. We might simply be trying to keep our heads above water; thus, when the person next to us feels hurt by our emphatic statement, it will pass our notice as we continue to ramble about the injustices of life.

I know what it is to taste disappointment and to feel that life is too difficult. I know what it is to attend a wedding during a painful season in my life and to feel sorry for the happy couple because they have no idea the depths of pain they will potentially experience in the future years of their relationship.

I ask of you, though, to take time to heal from the pain you feel and to do things that ignite joy, such as doing something you enjoy or by spending time in quiet, allowing God to show you his goodness and his restorative grace and breathe fresh life into your bones.

If your childhood experience of a father or mother was a painful one, then allow God to show you his love, to restore your heart, and to win your trust. I used to think of him as a fierce and angry God who was ready to punish me when I made a mistake, but I have found him to be the most-loving Father who wins my heart and trust with each new life experience.

The more you experience healing in the broken areas of your life, the more wisdom will be able to shine though, lending balance to your life and ensuring that you will not be affected by the hurtful words and actions of others as dramatically. You will instead be able to pause, reflect, and respond, and, at times, glean life-changing perspective and wisdom instead of feeling the need to react in anger or pain.

CHAPTER 9

Communicate, Do Not Assume

We demolish arguments and every pretension that
sets itself up against God, and we take captive
every thought to make it obedient to Christ.
—2 Corinthians 10:5, NIV

THE WAY I FELT ABOUT MYSELF IN MY YOUTH COLORED MY perspective and dramatically affected how I received comments from my husband.

I felt too vulnerable to ask for affirmation or let him know what I needed in our day-to-day life during our conversations. If I had asked, I have little doubt that this would have served our relationship well in our early years as opposed to us limping along for the many years we did, each guessing how to respond to one other.

This reminds me of miscommunications and assumptions in other areas too, such as the occasions when I was the wedding coordinator for some of my friends and family members over the years. There were several times when I realized, after the wedding, that some vital details were missing that did not show up until the event was in full swing.

On these occasions, there were tiny details I took for granted that the bride would tell me needed to be done, but they either did not think to convey them to me, or they simply expected that since I had coordinated before, I would know what should be done—such as when I thought my part in the wedding was done and found out later that there were some extra things others had to pitch in and help with when they were not expecting it to be their job. Although they did not complain to me, I sensed frustration from those who did not expect it.

There was also a time when I asked several questions, seeking clarity for my part in making things flow smoothly. I got to the rehearsal, where all who attended waited around for an extra hour because no one knew whose job it was to go ahead with the next step. Later, I realized it was my job, but due to a lack of communication, I wasted everyone's time. This was quite humbling for me, but it was also enlightening. I learned that I must insist on a thorough conversation with the bride so it is clear exactly what is expected of me. It also helped solidify the belief that, for a long-term, successful relationship between my husband and me, saying clearly what I wanted and needed was imperative.

This also brings to my memory a sweet friend of mine, who sometimes asked my opinion about her attire for special occasions. With the way she asked, I assumed that she did not like her attire, so I offered something for her to wear and she accepted. Later, it dawned on me that she was not asking me for help; she was asking if I thought she looked all right. I have often cringed to think about how I might have hurt her by my assumption.

This is also an area where a lot of pain is experienced between family members and friends. Much can get lost in translation, and our perspectives will affect how we hear something. For instance, when a friend relays something another person said to them that caused them great pain, but to my ears, it sounded completely different and I would not have felt hurt by what was said, it might be impossible for the one who feels hurt to look at things objectively because of his or her perspective.

It might take a level of vulnerability that you are uncomfortable with at times to be direct, but life will go much smoother and there will be much less guessing when you are willing to express yourself clearly. I understand today that the reason I found it difficult to ask for what I needed was because I feared my husband did not love me enough or find me worthy of the affirmations I wanted to hear. Couple that with refusing to accept compliments from him, it contributed to him struggling with how to give me what I needed.

Of course, there is never a guarantee that your spouse will give you what you ask for, and there are some who will simply refuse, but often, most will want to please you when they know what you want.

Although there is no guarantee that we will get what we ask for, we are certainly not going to get what we want if we do not ask for it in the first place. I spent many years in our relationship, hoping that my husband would recognize when I was stressed and offer to help me or figure out what I needed automatically and felt disappointed each time he did not. It would have helped us both tremendously if I had been able to express my wants and needs clearly.

As it turns out, when I ask for help, many times he chips in without complaint. This shows that he would have been willing to help all along, but because I kept hoping he would see I needed help and save me from having to ask, I caused us both frustrations over the years.

When we practice being direct and vulnerable, it gives those around us the freedom to do the same. It has become increasingly important to me to be exactly who I am. I do not care to keep up with what others do; neither do I want them to be impressed with who I am or pay attention to what I have. It is important to me that the janitor at the grocery store knows I value him or her and what he or she contributes to life just as much as I value the millionaire who creates jobs for the employees in the companies they own.

We often talk about the impact of peer pressure in school for our children, but it is just as much a part of adults' lives. As adults, we are often motivated to protect our reputations by how we act. At times, this causes us to be unkind to those we consider of less importance. In an era where there is intense motivation to be seen as someone important and to be an influencer on social media or have a large following in whatever we do, I find it increasingly important to unplug from the noise and make sure that what I am portraying in life is what I genuinely believe.

Each one of us desires to be seen and be known. Sometimes, this motivates us to be someone we really are not, to fit in with who we think are the right people. The more I see who I am to my heavenly Father and the more I realize there is only one me and that I am in competition with no one, it increasingly inspires me to live true to what I believe. If I do not fully live the life I have been given, it will go unlived.

I am finding that it is of immense value to be here, right now, today. If I am constantly concerning myself with what tomorrow holds, I am not here today. The more I am here, in this present moment, the more I value the connections with each person I interact with. We do not know what tomorrow holds. Being present now is all we have been given. Connecting with others, heart to heart, is what is important in life. The material things in life are a gift, but what worth do they have without people to love and be loved by?

From what I have heard over the past few years, we are living in an era where people are experiencing loneliness to a greater degree than ever before. This is likely because of social media, where it seems as though we are connecting because we interact with each other in written words, but many people are getting together less within our communities, and there is no substitute for in-person human connection. Taking time to get to know people and let them know you is such a beautiful gift. This inspires me increasingly, to let others know me, so the person next to me who is feeling lonely, might feel loved and seen too.

The lonely stranger will not care to know who I might be, whether I am someone important or what my status in life is, but when we connect heart to heart, strangers will know they are individuals who matter.

Letting others know that they are seen and heard is one of the most important things we do in life, but when we do not feel confident in who we truly are, we are so wrapped up in being worried about how we appear to others that we miss opportunities to love the one beside us. Be you.

CHAPTER 10

Tending My Garden

The Lord will guide you always; he will satisfy your
needs in a sun-scorched land and will strengthen
your frame. You will be like a well-watered
garden, like a spring whose waters never fail.
—Isaiah 58:11, NIV

Dear Kate,

One of the most valuable lessons in life I have
learned over the past few years is the beauty of tending
to my garden and watching life change for me and the
people around me. When I tend to my garden, it is
inevitable that it will spread into my neighbor's garden
and lend beauty to their yard as it grows and expands.

A few years ago, in the middle of one of those
moments when I felt I was at an impasse with my
husband and when I told God, "I do not think I have
it in me to choose us again," feeling frustrated and
hopeless, what I wanted in that moment was to escape
to a little cabin in a faraway wood and spend time with
just God and me.

What I heard from within was, "If nothing changes
ever again, what can I do to abide and grow right here?"

In that moment, I realized I can give this day another chance. I can take one more step. I can wriggle out of this unbearable cocoon and allow a softer, less prickly me to appear. When I hear words that reveal the unhealed pain in my heart, I will choose to hear through ears of love. I will listen without defense. I can do this much. If there is enough room for both of us to unpack what we each carry, there is enough room for this moment too.

Experiencing challenges like this, is incredibly beautiful. You might not be able to see it in the middle of these situations, but after you pass through the tight squeeze, being willing to come out softer, you will suddenly view life differently and become aware that it might not even have been the other person who needed to change. Instead, the gift for you was a new and fresh perspective.

I AM THE QUEEN OF MY CASTLE. WHEN I AM HAPPY, THE KING OF my castle, my husband, is happy. I set the tone for the environment in our home. Learning that I am the thermostat and not the thermometer has transformed the day-to-day temperature within our home. Instead of tiptoeing to test the temperature to see how my husband feels, I take personal responsibility to set the tone in the space I handle by confidently seeing well to the ways of my household. I am imperfect in this, and I am still learning how to be me, and this is OK.

The more I am aware I was given this husband, these children, and this home, whether by personal choice or by what felt like default at the time, the more I govern with grace and increasingly with peace. I choose this day to plant flowers, allow weeds to surface and lovingly uproot them, and let God's love within me to blossom. Each day, my garden becomes more beautiful, even though at times, when an especially difficult weed takes extra effort to uproot, it will still give eventually, and I will feel gratitude for the grace the uprooting gifts me with.

Dear Kate,

Take time to be in this moment. When you are feeling the most pain, take time to realize that you are strong enough to be here in this moment and walk through it. You have overcome every challenge to date. Take a little time to quit fixing yourself and just be here now. Take time to appreciate how the painful things have allowed your heart to come alive, sometimes in areas where you might have hardened it before, when you felt tired of feeling discomfort, yet you pressed on one more day.

You are strong enough. You were created for this life experience. You can do it. You are known, and you are seen. There is only one you. Live your life well. Know that in so many ways, your choices affect the outcome of your life. God is always at your back, supporting you and whispering in your ear, and he delights in who you are and loves to see life through your eyes, for it is a view that is unique to your eyes.

Although at times, you will feel there is no room for you and your voice, hear me when I say that there is a perfect space for the unique person you are. What do you want the world to know about you? Who are you? What do you love? How are you doing? I want to hear what you think.

Can you find it in your heart to feel gratitude for the most painful part of your journey so far? What has it taught you? What can you share with others that might encourage them to embrace the messiness in their lives? I repeat: you are strong enough and equipped to be you. If you do not know this yet, you will know it someday.

Love, Kate

Frequently, the traumas we experience in our early years drive us in life, where we either act in ways that are unhealthy for our bodies and ourselves, or we are driven to achieve things that nearly break us.

What would happen, Kate, if you were to allow to the healing oil of God's love to bathe your heart and create from a place of wholeness and peace with who you are? What would happen if you took the time to be here now and to abide and create from here?

Take time to sit and look at how the plants in your garden, that you see as weeds, have served you. The stubborn weed, while at times has caused you to be resistant to the change of seasons, has served its purpose once you realized that uprooting it serves you better, and watering some flowers, even when they appeared dead, breathed fresh color into your life. Take time to appreciate what some of these weeds have taught you. You typically work nonstop to improve your garden. How about you choose to sit quietly for a few moments and just watch the flowers grow?

Over the years, while we were growing together, my husband has always loved me, but he has not always seemed to like me. There were times in the unfolding of the flower I am that life proved challenging for both of us. As I developed, a new way of being together was needed for us both.

"I hate change!" my husband said emphatically one day, a few years back. What a challenge his wife is for him sometimes—the kind of wife who thrives on change and new experiences. His refusal to embrace change at times has given me the perfect space to grow into who I am, even though there have been times it has seemed like the exact opposite and like I might have chosen the wrong man to spend my life with.

A few years ago, in contemplating the place where I found myself, I asked God with a complete baring of my soul, "How do I know if I am supposed to be with this man, my husband?" What I heard was, if I look at the fruit the relationship with my husband has produced, it is obvious that he is the one who is perfect for me. To grow into the woman I am today, I needed to be willing to allow my husband to remain as he chose, while I filled and grew into the space that is mine to thrive in, by how I conduct myself each day. By my willingness to show up as I am, it created a happy space for us both. When I am happy, he is happy.

An important detail that was highlighted for me in the early years of our marriage was that of realizing the importance of protecting our marriage by paying attention to how we interact with and conduct ourselves around those of the opposite sex through all the seasons together of our lives.

I learned that men are often attracted first by how a woman looks and then pursue a relationship with her because of that attraction. Women, on the other hand, though they will notice a handsome man, are often attracted to a man through conversation with him and then develop a connection through getting to know him as an individual.

During the time of our separation, and humbling to admit, I felt extremely lonely. Because of my habit of letting life just happen as it will, this was a vulnerable and unsafe season for me to be in, especially because I had lost my footing on a personal and spiritual level. I am incredibly blessed that God protected me as he did, because much worse could have happened to me than did, since, in my naivety, I had no clue how the world outside of the box I was raised in worked.

Although I did ask for help from a few people, they themselves were not experienced in the challenges I was facing and were unable to give me sound advice. Had I known what I do now, though, I might have looked further for wise counsel to help me chart this new and unsure territory. Sometimes we do need to look for help outside the circle of people we know, but unfortunately, clear thinking was not a strength of mine at the time, and I was unaware that I could have been intentional with my choices.

During the time our marriage was broken to a degree that I thought unsalvageable, I invited someone outside our marriage to enter it by having a one-night stand. Not only was this unwise and unhealthy, but it also opened the door for harmful spiritual access to our relationship that added more trauma to the team of us, even though I did not realize we were a team at the time.

I had been taught about what sin was during all my growing-up years, but when it came to a time where I was looking for answers that eluded me and I was floundering in life, knowing what sin was did not help save me. I was on a downward spiral without knowing up from down.

Dear Kate,

I would like to share a few things about marriage that I find to be of vital importance. When you begin a relationship with the man you choose to spend your life with, he will have baggage just as you do. Without being aware of it, you expect the man of your dreams to sweep you off your feet and automatically know how to meet your needs and make you happy.

Although much of a relationship is still a mystery to you, it is important that you know that what you do will affect your husband as much as what he does affects you. You might not see yourself as a person of impact, but you are. Your husband is not created to make you happy. No human being is. A personal relationship with your heavenly Father will fill the void you think is supposed to be filled by your knight in shining armor. You might be taught that something is sin and therefore, it is wrong, but you should also know that, not only do some of your choices potentially cause your husband emotional harm; they can also spiritually harm the union you and your husband created with the joining of your hearts and bodies when your marriage began.

The joining you created is a sacred gift, and when you allow an extra person to intrude into your union, it invites the spiritual forces in the third person's life to tangle with your union and opens both you and your husband to spiritual forces that complicate who you are together, often in ways that one cannot see with the physical eye.

I understand that you were not taught the importance of this, but I am telling you what I have learned. If you and your husband are experiencing challenges in your relationship, or you think your relationship is over and you find your heart in a vulnerable place, it is ever so important to surround yourself with people you trust as opposed to spending time with people who are out to get what they want without regard for your well-being.

You must take responsibility for protecting your union even if you think it might be over. If you do think it might be over, it would be wise to exhaust every effort to find solutions to save it. Please do not invite an extra person in just because your relationship appears irredeemable. That is another way to live life by default instead of by intention. A marriage is not helped by adding another human being to it. Choose to honor and protect your relationship at any cost. If you find that you must end the relationship, at the very least, take time to spend alone with God and allow his love to heal your heart before you invite someone else into your life.

Love, Kate

When I spent time apart from my husband in the early years of our marriage, my heart felt profound grief and sadness over the loss of our marriage when I thought it might be finished forever. Because a person experiences intense grief and sadness when his or her marriage ends, it shows in a dramatic way just how powerful a union is between spouses and why it is more important than we often realize to treat each other as the sacred gifts from God that we are to each other and realize that we are not in competition with one another. We are on the same team.

I felt judgment from people who knew us both, for the choice I made in leaving. They felt strongly that my husband, who they knew as a great guy, did not deserve my actions. I agree, he did not deserve this, and it might have appeared that I did not care. But only if you could see into my heart could you have known how deeply it affected me and known the sadness I felt for him, despite that I felt unable to find a resolution. I hold no ill will for the judgment I felt from others because I know I have stood in judgment of others too. Thankfully, God worked beautiful grace and compassion in the areas of my heart where previously, judgment had been in charge.

I know, within our culture, we are taught from our youth that divorce is never a choice we should make, but I think we must consider that if infidelity takes place when a marriage is in trouble, spiritually, it is the same as joining in another union. I regret some of my choices immensely and have often cringed in shame about my actions and felt sad for the harm they brought to our union. At the same time, I have chosen to allow God to heal and redeem the harm my choices caused us.

Today, I meet myself with compassion and forgiveness. I am humbled to realize that I was completely lost at the time and had no idea how important choosing with intention was instead of living by default.

I asked God to release and dissolve each harmful cord that entangled my marriage from my union with another person, and I chose to forgive myself as my heavenly Father has. I have given myself grace where before, I lived with guilt, judgment, and shame for my choices.

Today, the experience is far removed from me, and I have no desire to return to it. I am grateful for the restoration and redemption of the broken paths I have walked along. These choices imparted valuable life lessons to me, and because of redemption, have potentially enabled me to help those I share my experience with.

In my youth, without realizing how judgmental I was, I would have been the first one in line to condemn someone else for the very choices I eventually made. How wonderful is God who, when we make choices that potentially destroy our lives, through repentance—which means to think differently, thus, we do differently—he redeems each experience when we are willing to agree with him and meet ourselves with the same compassion and grace he meets us with. He truly is a redeeming Father.

One of the most valuable things I have learned to support and protect my marriage is, when in a group setting, if for some reason the group disperses and I find myself alone with only another man left in conversation, I will very quickly find a reason to excuse myself and leave the room as well.

I want to protect and honor my relationship with my husband; therefore, it is easy for me to make this decision each time to show both him and others that who we are together is sacred to me. There is a wall in my heart that only he is allowed access through.

The grace that has been worked in my heart through almost twenty-eight years of marriage is a profound gift. I feel gratitude for the wonderful person my husband is. If I had given up on us somewhere within these years, I would have missed both the person I have discovered in myself and the man I discovered in my husband.

I have been blessed with a husband who is steady, loyal, and anchored. He has chosen me each time, again, regardless of the cost to his heart. What greater qualities to discover in the man I married, than those that allow me to blossom exactly as I should, even if it might have taken a few replantings over the years and might take even more in the future.

I have learned that a living, breathing relationship is ever-changing in my marriage just as it is with my heavenly Father. My life experiences have shown me that the more I learn, the less I know. May my heart be ever pliable and soft as it becomes increasingly resilient.

CHAPTER 11

The Words You Speak

Learn to be OK with people not knowing your side
of the story. You have nothing to prove to anyone.
—Anonymous

Dear Kate,

You know how it bothers you when you realize you
were being discussed by others? This is likely to happen
through every season of your life. Live anyway. Be true
to who you are. Let not the fear of what others might
perceive of you keep you from living your life. You
know the quote, "live by applause, die by criticism"?
Let it inspire you each day to live true to who you are.

In the same way, you dislike being discussed by
others. Have you considered that you discuss the lives
of others as well? Even if, most of the time when you
discuss others, it might be coming from a caring place,
it does not mean that if they heard it, they would feel
it was caring. You might think you understand them
and have a good perspective of who they are and of
how they view life, but be mindful of treading gently
in this area too.

Love, Kate

WE CAN BE SURE WE KNOW WHAT IS WHAT, BUT BECAUSE OF our own lives' experiences, we are still vulnerable to seeing things incorrectly, and sometimes because of unhealed trauma, we react to others in a way that feels justified but is really an automatic reaction to the trauma instead of a right response.

From an early age, I have often been able to notice what others are feeling, and this has proven to make life difficult for me at times. It has taken time and effort to discover what feelings are mine and which are someone else's when it comes to feeling things in the company of others.

Because I feel tension when it is in the room, I often notice when others are upset by seeing their almost unreadable expressions even when no words are spoken. I am increasingly aware that it is important not to comment on these things to others so I do not affect how they feel about someone else. Most times, discussing how others are doing does not improve their lives just because I see something, even if I am correct. I do not wish to make others feel more vulnerable than they already are or to step into their personal space without invitation.

Wisdom teaches me there are many things that do not require my commentary. There are plenty of occasions when other people will discuss you, but only the opinions of those who wish you well and want the best for you matter. They are the ones who will contribute to your life in ways that improve your experiences as opposed to those who feel they are in competition with you.

Also, remember this, which is a variation of the quote: "If you knew how little people thought about you, you would not care what they think about you." To me, this means that most people are wrapped up in their own lives and do not have time to pay attention to yours except to comment on it at times. It also reminds me of the value in the quote, "Those rowing their own boats will not have time to watch how you row yours."

Dear Kate,

I have spent too much of my life concerned about what other people think of me. Know this: everybody will have a different opinion. You can try to do everything perfectly, but someone will still judge you and comment that you are doing something wrong. Let this motivate you. Do not wait for the eighty-year-old you to say, "I wish I had truly lived."

Remember this truth: those who discuss others with you will also discuss you with others. Even if you have a habit of not repeating what you know someone else told you in secret, this does not mean another person will honor this when it comes to something you discuss with him or her. Something I have noticed in life is that some people are information carriers. You might consider them friends, and they may consider you their friend, but anything you discuss with them will be carried to someone else, and this does not always bring a desirable outcome.

Because of this truth, I find it valuable not to tell others a lot of personal things about my life. It is best for people not to know what you have. If you do not care what people think of you, you will not be motivated to share things that give them ammunition to share about you unnecessarily. When people you know tell you about all the goings-on of other people, it is likely they will do the same thing to you in conversation with others. Exercise wisdom in sharing with others.

Love, Kate

"Be the woman who fixes another woman's crown
without telling the world it was crooked."
—Anonymous

Dear Kate,

You know how hurt your heart felt when an acquaintance said this person was discussing with someone else the possibility that the reason you made observations in your book the way you did was because you had dealt with certain family dynamics for so long that it was your way of acting out. You know how much it hurts that this person could think you were trying to hurt those you love? Please allow this to be a simple reminder for you to be thoughtful of the observations you make or repeat about others in the future. You might think your words are innocent and harmless, but it might hurt their hearts deeply. Good intentions in this way do not hold much weight. The person who is the object of your discussion will feel hurt that someone would see him or her in this light. I am sure I have been guilty of this many times throughout my life.

A few statements I have begun to repeat regularly that help me release guilt and forgive myself and others are, "I forgive others as they forgive me. I forgive myself as others forgive me, and I forgive myself as my heavenly Father forgives me."

Love, Kate

Women in general often discuss other people. It is something that comes naturally. When we discuss people and we have an opinion about another person, our opinion may be right, but it might also be wrong. Therefore, when we make observations, whether they are true or not, they might affect how someone else sees a person or how the person feels about him- or herself when the individual hears the observations.

I have noticed at times that, while out to dinner with my husband or a friend at lunch, I often overhear women having discussions about other women. Often, the words are angry, frustrated, or unkind. It has caused me to examine my own habits. I think many times we secretly think that if someone else does something worse than what we do or does something we would never do, then we feel better about our own lives. We may gloss right over something we know we should not do when we see another person doing something we think is worse.

Many years ago, when my husband and I were separated and my husband shared something about me with a mutual friend, the friend repeated it to someone else, and it made its way back to me. It made me sound like a heartless villain, and this hurt my heart terribly. I am sure this person did not know that what was said would be carried back to me, and in all probability, the individual likely did not consider the weight of these words.

It caused me to reflect on my own choice of words. I am sure I have been careless over the years and commented on things concerning others without much regard for the person being discussed, and I have no idea how many careless comments or observations have been carried back to the people being discussed or how much I hurt their hearts. May I always remember to hold the hearts of others gently on my tongue.

> Dear Kate,
>
> You know how much it bothers you when people come talk to you about another person about things you cannot fix. Remember when you came to the realization of how important it is to you to talk to the person these conversations concern when there is a problem. One of the most important things in friendship and family relationships is to talk to the person the problem concerns.
>
> Be gentle in discussing another person with friends and family. You know how much it hurts your heart when you hear that someone discussed something you did or thought or said without checking in with you. You feel violated when you hear that someone mentioned they saw a certain problem with you, when you think there is no truth to this whatsoever. It also hurts when there really is truth to their observations. For the times when there is truth to these statements, and even if it hurts, receive it with grace, take time to reflect, and allow it to soften your heart.
>
> How often in times past might you have done this to others? I do not ask this to condemn or criticize you, but I ask it as a reminder for you to be gentle and always speak to the person involved and not to others,

who can listen but not fix the problem. Sometimes a person will say something about you that is completely baseless because of his or her own perspective. Learn not to be offended when someone mentions something he or she sees in you, and the conversation makes its way back to you.

If what these people say is true, allow God's love to change your heart; if it is not true, let it be another reminder not to do the same to others.

Love, Kate

There are times when we are vulnerable within familial relationships to those who refuse to heal, and instead pass blame on others, weaponizing what they have learned in therapy. This can seem like confirmation to us who come from a culture that tends to think only people with extreme problems or mental health struggles go to a counselor. Each one of us, in different periods of our lives, can receive help from good counsel, and it does not mean there is a major problem with a person who decides to see one. I am the first to admit that I have a major appreciation for good therapists.

A good therapist or counselor will be a safe place to voice your thoughts when you find yourself experiencing challenges that seem insurmountable within your marriage or are experiencing great difficulty in dealing with childhood trauma. Therapists will suggest solutions for the things you are struggling with. A therapist is only helpful, though, if he or she helps you challenge your perspective over time, and where you are making decisions that do not serve you well, this person will invite you to see things differently. A therapist who supports you staying locked in an unhealthy place is not helpful or good for you.

It is my experience that, at times, people who rely entirely on a therapist to deal with relationships and learn a lot of the words therapists use, develop the habit of using it to leverage their relationships with family members in painful situations. These individuals may not even be aware they are doing this, but because they learn the language, they feel they have changed and lack the ability to see that they simply adapted to a new language but are still functioning in their broken states.

Boundaries are important, and many of us are raised without knowing what healthy boundaries are. It is incredibly important to develop healthy boundaries, and not only does it require us to learn new ways of responding to life but it also allows us to be changed from the inside out.

During times when there is turmoil and unrest within the family or in the world with varying degrees of opinions on subjects, it is my experience that those who are well-versed in therapy without having put the effort in to heal their traumas, tend to set boundaries and take it a step further but accept a relationship only on their terms.

When a person with a differing opinion says something the person in therapy does not like, his or her response may be to refuse having further conversation at all. It is possible that this is all the individual feels capable of handling now, but hopefully he or she will seek further aid in healing to interact in a healthy way.

In the families that God placed us with, how will we heal the dysfunction and unhealthy habits in our family lineage, as opposed to healing it, if we leave our families? and when I say healing our family instead of leaving, I do not mean that you should stay if there is harm being done or a religion being practiced to the point that you cannot freely live by your own conviction.

I also understand that there are times in the middle of intense family struggles, that each one of us may feel the need to take a break from spending time with some family members for a while. Sometimes, spending a little time apart can help us to see each other through a new lens and see the situation from an objective viewpoint.

What I am saying is that much of the time in today's world, if we do not like something about someone else, we tend to show him or her the door and put the person out of our lives because the individual is difficult. It has been my experience that every person I have found to be difficult has had something beautiful to teach me even though it did not feel beautiful in the unfolding. In fact, it brought me to moments where I thought I could not take much more pain, but by sitting with it long enough and challenging my own perspectives, I was able to give the other person room for his or her views and perspectives and allow myself to retain what is healthy and balanced.

I have heard the saying, "If someone no longer serves you, put him or her out of your life." Yes, sometimes that may be the healthy choice, but sometimes we put people out of our lives who would teach us an important life lesson if we would simply give it time; otherwise, we are presented with an opportunity in the future to learn the life lesson again.

It is one of the main things that affects couples in relationships. It is my experience that a long-term marriage will have quite a few moments that feel like they are going to break you. In the process, if you allow it, these experiences will show you everything about yourself that is filled with flawed views and perspectives that may otherwise go unchanged, or you will get to be challenged by it again in the next relationship unless you take time to heal first.

There have been many occasions when my husband said something to which I took great offense when he meant it completely innocently, and by healing the hurts that fueled my perspective, I learned to hear what he said instead of projecting my feelings and lack of being enough on him.

In allowing grace for yourself in the journey, you can allow your husband time and space to walk his path and heal his wounds. By working together, you can support each other to become emotionally healthy. When you are looking for the best in each other and want to come together even though you misunderstand each other at times, and when times are so difficult that you do not know if you can try again, when you at least set the intention that you want to be open to trying, this situation truly has a way of working itself out for both of you.

Dear Kate,

May I tell you about something I find incredibly important? It is about the use of blanket statements. This is a term I use to describe how people throw everyone under one blanket, especially people who they disagree with and use this statement to try to prove why they themselves are right.

When using a blanket statement, you will always hurt someone. Yes, you might get to stick it to people you disagree with or who you are angry at, but for every blanket statement you give, there are many people of the same or similar opinion as you, who do not fit under that blanket. When you call out another person for being judgmental, are you not also standing on the throne of judgment?

I think back on my life and recall various occasions when, in frustration, I made a blanket statement, and when I revisit each time it happened, I can see that I hurt others by my opinionated and frustrated outburst.

When fighting to be right, we feel justified by our stances in life, and when we can call out those of opposing views, though we may not want to tell them directly, if we say it where they can see or hear us, we have said our righteous piece and happily continue the paths we are on, relieved we got our points across, all without realizing it leaves a bitter sound in the ear of the recipient or bystander.

I have noticed this also leeches into the conversations between women, concerning men. Do we consider how much it hurts the individual when we lump all men together by our negative experiences with one or a few different men who have been in our lives? Throughout history, women have discussed the men in their lives with each other. Sometimes, the men being discussed walk up in the middle of the conversation, and I cannot help but think this causes them great pain, just as it would us when being discussed in a less-than-flattering manner, even if the men will not admit it.

Becoming aware of this a few years ago prompted me to be increasingly mindful of the things I say about my husband. If I complain to my friends about my frustrations with my husband, they will understand and will respond with similar frustrations in most cases, but does this serve us well? We do not like it when word travels back to us about an unkind remark our husbands might have made about us. I have heard it said, "Let the words you speak to others concerning your husband, upon reaching his ears, always be kind ones."

I am not referring to the times you are having trouble in your relationship where you seek out a trusted friend and confidant from whom to get feedback. A devoted friend will never bash your husband, even if you do.

A loyal friend will listen to you and suggest the possibility that your husband has a different view on the subject or that he might be unable to handle what you are feeling on an emotional level, and even at times, share ideas about how you might connect with your spouse with a new perspective.

Sometimes, the sisters or friends in your life who are in a healthy place themselves are the best people to aid you in working through relationship challenges because they will challenge your perspective in an area where you might be blinded by pain.

Love, Kate

I am most grateful to be blessed with sisters who love us both and who support my relationship with my husband to the extent that they will always offer objective views to seek the outcome serving both my husband and me well. To have a trusted group of women in my life who encourage and challenge my perspective in all areas of life is a gift I value tremendously.

It has quite often been in this very mirror of wise counsel that I have been challenged by blanket statements I have made and have been reminded to think again about the conclusion I have arrived at through painful experiences. Just because life and relationships have proven our perspectives right many times over does not mean it is the correct solution to arrive at. Sometimes, the wise counsel of others will help us to see things differently and contribute to our ability to live life healthier, especially in our relationships with our husbands.

CHAPTER 12

Love Through Misunderstanding

The Lord appeared to us in the past, saying: "I
have loved you with an everlasting love; I have
drawn you with everlasting kindness.
—Jeremiah 31: 3, NIV

SOMETHING I HAVE NOTICED OVER THE COURSE OF MY LIFE IS THAT
we humans have such an intense desire to be understood that
when we feel misunderstood, we tend to complain or lash out
at others. One of the secrets I have learned is that when you surrender
the need to be understood, it brings an incredible amount of peace into
your life. When you are OK with others not understanding you, you
no longer live and work to gain the approval of others.

When you no longer mind whether others agree with you, and
if it turns out they do not agree, it does not threaten your existence;
you understand that you simply do not connect with them, and that is
OK. Being aware of this enables me to set them free to walk their own
journeys, knowing it is not up to me to figure out who is right and who
is wrong. God takes care of and works things out for each one of us.

This also encourages me to stay in my lane and be OK with
connecting only with those I should. I will be friendly to everyone, but
this does not mean it is intended for me to be a close friend to everyone.

Requiring that I become everyone's friend is more pressure than I feel capable of handling, especially when I forget that I am not responsible for their lives' choices and begin to carry them emotionally.

Because I feel deeply, I must exercise wisdom for when to give, or my past's tendency to give more than I am capable of and have nothing left for my husband and children, who are my priority, will show itself again. If I spread myself thin to help others, I will be unable to efficiently do my primary job well. It has taken a lot of practice for me to learn how to say no.

> Growth is often uncomfortable, messy, and full
> of feelings you were not expecting, but trust me,
> it is necessary. Feel through it and smile through
> it. You have survived every other difficult day,
> and you will make it through this one too.
> —Anonymous

Dear Kate,

When there is someone in your life who challenges your perspective, take that as a gift. People who tell you only what you want to hear are not going to help you grow. It is those who ask you questions and challenge your perspective sometimes who allow you to see how you are tripping up in your own life.

If you are not concerned with being understood, and instead you are concerned about learning what is right, good, and best for you, then it is OK if no one understands you. When you know who you are, you no longer need someone to clarify things for you, and you no longer need someone to listen to you just so you can be reassured of your own standing. Be courageous by inviting God's love into the areas that trip you up and exchange them for more freedom to be the authentic person you came into this life to be.

Love, Kate

We take on many things as children; we are taught, and these things become a part of our belief systems. Growing often means shedding those things and challenging the perspectives we currently have, based on our experiences. We often judge life and others by our own experiences. This does not mean that our perspectives are correct, since we are often affected by our experiences in different areas that we are unaware of.

Always allow others to challenge your perspective. If your perspective is still the same after being challenged, that is fine. I have often found that, by having my perspective challenged, I end up experiencing freedom to a greater measure; it transforms my life and reminds me that I alone am accountable for how I live my life.

It used to serve me well when I was waiting for God to spontaneously reveal and drop my calling into my life. When someone shared with me that I would be doing something specific in the future, in the form of a word of knowledge, I accepted the belief that things would suddenly be dropped into my life one day. This served me well until I realized that sometimes, when someone shares a word of knowledge about something specific for us, it is a promising idea for us to give attention to and develop our skills in that area, especially if it connects with something in our hearts.

When we are waiting for a promise to be realized, it does not mean that we should not be doing anything in the meantime. It means that it is a great idea to pursue the things we are interested in, the things that are in our hearts, and as we go about our lives, more will be revealed to us. Remember that saying, "A ship cannot be turned while it is still docked in the harbor"? Do what you know to do with what is in your hand right now.

> Dear Kate,
>
> When you are living in a way that affects your own life in a negative manner, do not be surprised when things come along to disrupt your life. Sometimes, obstacles come up to show you your blind spots and to give you the opportunity to exchange your way of being for a way that much better serves you. Be open,

even when you feel threatened by a new idea. Know that you have God's help to show you what is best for you.

Love, Kate

I used to feel frustrated and angry at people in my life who would suggest this and that for my health and for my body. It made me angry that they would discuss me while I was not there. The truth is, I felt vulnerable and did not want anybody to discuss my issues. I wanted to be in control of what others thought of me. I do not like it when people think they must fix me (says the girl who is a recovering fixer!).

In reflection, how often do I think that way about someone else? How often do I see a problem in someone else's life and think that if he or she could just see clearly in this area, the individual's life would be infinitely better? Obviously, others can see the blind spots in my life too. I just do not like it when they tell me what I need to do or suggest things that I need to fix.

If I am not scared of being vulnerable, what do I have to lose by allowing myself to be transparent and vulnerable? Often, when I feel that someone else is trying to change me, I want to ask the individual about this and that in his or her own life. But then I am reminded that, when someone notices something that is not working for me, it is a gift for me when this comes into focus, whether because of another person or through my own realization.

There have been many sweet reminders in my life to let go of the need to defend myself. One of the most challenging and rewarding things I have learned to date is that, by allowing intimacy in the form of being known by others, it helps me be OK with being known exactly as I am, flaws and all, and I increasingly surrender my desire to hide as new areas come into focus in my life.

Sometimes love will disrupt my dysfunction so I can be known to others in a more open and loving way. Yes, I could protect myself and not allow others to know me or see me. But to truly live, can I afford to hide? Can I afford to be withdrawn? I do not think that still being hidden will serve me well in this life. How will it help me if someone thinks well of me, but they do not know me? How much more is it worth for someone to know me, flaws and all, and valuing me as a human being?

CHAPTER 13

Misjudged

Be completely humble and gentle; be patient,
bearing with one another in love.
—Ephesians 4:2, NIV

Dear Kate,

You know how it bothers you tremendously when someone makes a mistake or questions your intentions in a situation? You know how you have lost sleep obsessing about how someone interpreted something you said, worrying about whether the person understands where you are coming from and being afraid you have offended him or her?

I cannot tell you how much peace you will experience when you understand that you cannot control how other people experience you. When you decide to be OK with letting others see you exactly as they choose to, without feeling defensive or worrying about your reputation, this truth will change your life dramatically. One of the most challenging times is to keep your mouth closed when you experience someone in an incredibly painful way, and the next person discredits your experience by telling you why that person is excused because he or she knows the individual and is a good judge of character, and thus the person's intentions were good, without doubt.

I would like to give you an example. Several years ago, during a time when I was feeling especially raw and vulnerable, a friend sent me a message to tell me about a conversation wherein my friend felt I had caused harm by the words I had spoken. When words like betrayal and sacred trust broken went with the message, my carefully constructed and controlled world, where I am always kind, fell apart.

For the next few days, I cried endless tears, could not sleep, and my stomach hurt too much to eat. Some of the thoughts racing through my mind endlessly were, *How could someone think me capable of betrayal? I have only ever done everything in my power to love others and build people up. Am I that blind? Is there something wrong with me? Am I unkind?*

As I trudged through the next few days, I tried to open my bruised heart to examine the conversation objectively. Little by little, I reviewed the suggested accusations I experienced as though they were true: If I betrayed, then I will begin today with being trustworthy. If I broke sacred trusts, then I will begin today with keeping sacred trusts. If I am unkind, then I will begin today with being kind.

It gradually set me free to be exactly as I am, a person who lives in part to love others and who loves to give gifts and brighten the day of each person I meet. When I reviewed these accusations replaying in my mind with, "If I am this person, then this is who I am. I will begin anew right here, right now," to say I felt humbled by this experience would be an understatement. It cracked a major chink in my carefully constructed view that that I am perceived as kind and loving by others. Whether I was unkind did not matter so much as letting go of the need to control how others experienced me.

Love, Kate

I HAVE ALWAYS DONE MY BEST NOT TO INVOLVE OTHERS UNNECESSARILY when interacting with a person who was less than positive or who might affect the reputation of said person. Carefully, and looking to tread softly while in conversation with a friend, I expressed how I had felt misunderstood and had experienced great pain with a recent interaction with another friend. My confidant quickly explained to me that this person was a mutual friend, and thus my pain was caused by my perspective, and not by our mutual friend.

My heart was squeezed in pain by this response. I felt hurt that my confidant, who I thought knew me well, quickly excused the actions of my friend, and confirmed that the friend's words to me were justified. This interaction taught me about perspective. We might each have a different one. We also might agree with another person's perspective based on our individual experiences, but the challenge comes when we hear things from someone else's point of view and receive an invitation to see things differently.

It also taught me the importance of not discrediting someone's experience just because I view things differently. Until I interact with an individual, I cannot know how someone else will experience him or her, and at times, my experience with an individual will be different than the next person's, making it impossible for me to understand the next person's experience. Here is where reminding ourselves to love each other even when we are unable to understand the other person's perspective, comes into play.

How we experience others is a gift. Sometimes it is a painful gift, but it is one that works beautiful grace in areas of our hearts that might otherwise go unchanged, areas that we want to grow in love but might not know how until life hands us the opportunity in an uncomfortable exchange.

It is exceedingly difficult when you feel misjudged by others. But when you reexamine the experience and it does a beautiful work in your heart, does it really matter if someone thinks your perspective was wrong? What is significant, though, is the importance of coming to a place of peace with what happened and being able to truly forgive the person with whom you had the painful experience.

Dear Kate,

May I remind you here, in the same manner you want others to know that, despite the imperfect delivery, your intentions are to be kind, and that the friend you felt hurt by might also have had good intentions? It might be as simple as the idea that your friend experienced what you said through a lens of pain, and thus the person responded from that perspective. And though the delivery caused you pain, the individual's intention was to set right something your friend perceived to be wrong. If for some reason your friend had unkind intentions, this experience in making your heart soft, pliable, and less defensive still proved to be a beneficial life-changing lesson.

Whether I play the part of Jesus or the part of Pharaoh, may I allow others to experience me exactly as they will. I am not responsible for how they see me or how they experience me. I love them and I want to take care of them, but if I am truly going to live, I cannot worry about controlling how other people see me. I release them to experience me exactly as they do. Something I say to myself often is, "I release every person to experience me as he or she will." I shall hold myself to a standard of grace and not perfection. I shall also hold others to a standard of grace and not perfection.

Love, Kate

CHAPTER 14

Disappointed

But those who hope in the Lord will renew their
strength. They will soar on wings like eagles; they will
run and not grow weary; they will walk and not faint.
—Isaiah 40:31, NIV

FROM WHAT I HAVE HEARD, THE YEAR 2020 WAS AN INTENSE YEAR for most people. It certainly was a challenging one for me. In January, my daughter bought her own home. At the end of the day that we got her moved in, after saying our goodbyes, we left—my husband got into his truck, and I got in mine. I mulled over the day and, without getting too deep into what I was feeling, I accepted this new experience.

Lying in bed a few hours later, my husband remarked, "Somewhere across town, just east of us, our daughter is starting life out on her own." This got my thoughts racing, which I had previously thought were under control, and as I prayed for my daughter's protection that night, feeling anxious that she was on her own, the peace that both of my children were home after school or work each day eluded me, but I eventually fell into a fitful sleep.

I woke up the next day with a sore throat, and for the next thirteen days, I was sicker than I could remember ever being before. There were a few tears each day, with the loss my heart felt over my daughter leaving. I was absolutely thrilled for her and impressed by her decision to strike out on her own, which highlighted the independent person she is. I reminded myself repeatedly that I would have thought myself capable at her age, but somehow, I felt older at age twenty-three than the child who I had carried beneath my heart for nine months, gave birth to, and had raised from child to adult, was now.

In March, I started off with an online business and marketing class and felt confident in my footing, and then the lockdowns began. With the many years of research about health I have done over the years, I quickly developed an opinion that allowed me to see through the harmful fear campaign I felt was being marketed to the world.

This opinion enabled me to focus on building a stronger immune system by what I put into my body. I researched which supplements would support my immune system, began taking them daily, and intentionally went to the grocery store at least once a week, so my body kept being introduced to the germs floating around in my community in small doses. I did not wear a mask since from what I had read, the virus was so minuscule as to be able to go right through most masks except for those available within the medical community, especially those fitted to an individual, and because of what I had read, I believe long-term mask-wearing makes people vulnerable to pneumonia and other lung health issues, since fresh air in our lungs is essential for our bodies to receive enough oxygen to thrive.

I continued to go without until the doors were guarded with people demanding a mask be worn to be allowed entry. I bought a see-through lace mask online and wore it for the duration of the stores' demands.

I do not say this lightly, because I am aware that to many people, I was being irresponsible for choosing to live this way. I share it because this is what I believed was the best choice for me, with how to respond to what was happening in the world, and I find it increasingly difficult to live any other way than by my personal convictions, even when it might offend people I love and care about deeply.

It was painful for me, a person who cares deeply about others, to be accused of being selfish because of my personal decision to go without a mask and to refuse the vaccine that people said, by getting it, would prove I care about others. I had to grow yet again by doing what I believed was right despite others thinking I was wrong. My heart bled often for the many people who lost loved ones during this time.

Due to the research I had done, I struggled to deal with the overwhelming fear pervading the earth, which I felt intensely. It was difficult to go to the store each week and to see people in the aisles avoid eye contact, and when someone did meet my eyes, the fear I saw was overwhelming. I felt angry with the nefarious forces I believed were working behind the scenes. I continually tried to let go of the anger I felt so as not to take it out on innocent people paralyzed by the fear they were experiencing because of what they were being told. I felt it on a personal level due to the vastly different views my daughter and I had on the subject.

I took for granted that since we are family, I would still get to see my daughter, even if I had to stay away from others, but I learned quickly that I was not allowed to see her because I did not properly quarantine, and therefore, it was thought I might unknowingly make others sick. For the next year and a half, I cried daily for the separation the response to the virus brought to my life. I had hugged my daughter daily before she moved out, and just when I had adjusted to seeing her occasionally, all physical contact ceased.

I grieved intensely, my heart feeling as though I had lost her forever because I could not see the possibility that this separation might be temporary.

Because of our drastically different views and a few attempts to have conversations that did not bring us understanding—which I freely admit that my contribution to our conversation was delivered imperfectly—I became my daughter's enemy, and days and sometimes weeks passed without even phone contact.

I grieved for the elderly who lived alone and who were not allowed to have visits from their loved ones. I cried for those who died alone without the gift of their loved ones' presence as they passed from this life to the next. I felt angry when my daughter chose the entire world over me. Logically, I understood that she made her decisions based on what she felt was best, and that it was not personal, but it felt oh so personal.

My daughter is an amazing, compassionate, and courageous young woman. I know few who are stronger than she is, but as her mama, I needed her and felt devastated when I felt I had lost her. I know it was intended for children to leave home, but my heart was unable to see logic and hold onto hope for the possibility that we might be reconciled someday.

Growing up Amish, one of the things I learned is that we are a clannish people. We stick with those we know, and it is a wonderful thing to have community support in all we do and in everything we face. But on the other side is the not-so-good part, where we tend to associate only with those who are like-minded and cast out those who develop an unfamiliar perspective.

Having the experience of my daughter seeing life through a completely different lens than mine gave me the wonderful gift of looking at life through the eyes of others in a way I might otherwise have refused to, had it not been forced upon me. I wrestled daily with this painful gift for more than a year. It felt like I had tasted a literal bite of disappointment and that I was unable to shake it off.

When friends shared about something they did with their children during this season, my heart squeezed in pain. When another friend's child had a baby, my heart squeezed some more. Joy eluded me, and loneliness tried to consume me. I was aware I was not handling things well, and this did not sit well with me. I had always handled things. This was unacceptable, and alas, I asked how I could go on like this.

As I went to bed one evening, tears quietly squeezing from my closed eyes, I whispered, "Father, I am not doing so good." I remember it well, especially because I thought this was not proper English. At once, I saw a picture of myself treading water. My heart filled with compassion. I realized in that moment that, although I might not be thriving, if I saw my friend treading water, I would not berate her, and I would not ask her to handle things differently, let alone do better. I would offer my help, and I would love her right where she was, so I chose to meet myself there, just as I was. In that very moment, I met myself with compassion. Though I was disappointed that I was not handling things better and I was not as strong as I had hoped, I let it be enough.

I decided to take a break from social media. I felt the need to get quiet and allow my heart to deal with the pain on a personal level instead of demanding it help the rest of the world get through the trauma the year 2020 brought. I struggled with my decision since I was a helper and a fixer, but suddenly, I could not even fix myself, and I needed to take care of myself first. This was a first for me.

Throughout this time, I often mentioned to God that I was uncomfortable that joy eluded me. It was not OK with me that disappointment felt like it had taken root in my heart. Many evenings, I would look up funny videos online to make myself laugh because I had discovered that laughter is the right medicine at times.

Gradually, my heart began to beat again. I began to feel joy with what was. I accepted that my daughter's perspective would serve her well, just as mine served me. I let go of the need to protect her. Instead of praying endlessly for God to save her from a perspective I felt was harming her, I began to pray for grace, strength, and courage for her journey with him. I kept telling myself, "Come on, Mama, let go."

I slowly came to the awareness; I had raised her to the best of my ability. It was time to trust her to do life on her own. I am sure there are many mothers who handle their children leaving home better than I did. I humbly admit that I limped through the letting-go process.

Today, my heart is at peace with where we are. Life looks different than the one in my dreams, but then, why would it not? My dreams are not my daughter's dreams. My daughter is a gift who was given to me as a baby to nurture and grow up, and then to set free to fly on her own wings. What a sweet gift she has been to partner with me in revealing important life lessons such as embracing those who think completely differently, while realizing that we all do life differently, but we also have a lot more in common than we think, if we will but take time to see through each other's lenses without fear and judgment.

By letting this be an experience where I practiced letting go of feeling like I must go at life alone, I let go of the need to be more than enough and of handling things by allowing myself to ask for support from my husband at various times. His encouragement reinforced my belief that I could accept this new normal, that life would go on, and that sometimes, different is good too.

I learned at an early age to be strong. This was a time of learning to be soft. Sometimes, being strong is also being soft.

CHAPTER 15

The Little Things

Rejoice always, pray continually, give thanks in all
circumstances; for this is God's will for you in Christ Jesus.
—1 Thessalonians 5:16–18, NIV

Dear Kate,

When you care about something, know that God
does too. Nothing is too small for his attention. Just
like every other human being, you are also uniquely his
beloved. Many times, we feel we do not matter much.
We feel insignificant, and we are OK with the belief
that God is good for others, but we are not sure he is
good for us. We are often quick to think that we are
too flawed and too unlovable to be heard and seen, but
God cares intimately about each moment, each day, and
each challenge we experience.

Love, Kate

A S A CHILD, I WAS AFRAID OF GOD. I HEARD ABOUT HOW HE
loves us, but we also learned that he was filled with wrath, and
it is only because Jesus died for us that God can stand us. I felt
safe with Jesus but was afraid of God.

When I came to know that the Bible says, "If you really know me, you will know my father as well. From now on, you do know him and have seen him" (John 14:7, NIV). Jesus said, "anyone who has seen me has seen the father" (John 14:9, NIV). This tells me Jesus came to reveal the Father's heart to his children.

Getting to know my heavenly Father's heart helped me understand that God loves me the same as Jesus does. It helped me trust God, and through that process, he became a loving Father to me, the best, loving, heart-winning Father you could ever meet. In a time when what it means to have a father is missing in many children's lives, getting to know our heavenly Father's heart is imperative and will result in restoring the hearts of the children to their fathers and vice versa.

Pray for your children, for their present and futures and for their potential life partners. Ask God to lead them to the people who are right for them. Do not insist that their paths look like you think they should. When you ask for God's guidance for them, trust that he will see to your children's well-being.

When my husband left the church of his youth, I have no doubt that it was an incredibly painful time for his parents who had hoped he would stay in the church, marry an Amish girl, and raise his family just as they did. When my husband left, they needed to deal with a completely new and unique way of life where he was concerned. As a family, we tried to wade through this separate way of life, and it took many years to adjust.

When their son married me, it dashed any hopes they had of his eventual return, and although I was raised Amish too, it was not what they had hoped for in a marriage for their son. Because of their inability to accept their son's choice of a different path, they missed a close relationship with him for the rest of their lives and might not have realized just how amazing their son was. It would have been a wonderful gift to them to be able to know their son well.

In looking back over the years, I also think because of the pain we felt in being rejected by family for the decision to leave the church of our youth, at first as individuals and then as a married couple, it is likely that the chip we carried on our shoulders contributed at times to the lack of close relationships we might have developed if we had been able to be seen through our pain and had the courage to be more vulnerable in conversations with them.

We might not know how, but in each challenging situation we find ourselves, being open and willing to try again enables us to connect in new ways that we might originally have thought impossible. I felt sad for this part of our journey, but at the same time, it was one of those valuable life lessons I feel incredibly grateful for, because it helped me to understand the importance of being open to others when they choose a different path than mine, even when my path is the right or best one.

I had naively thought I would not have to experience the pain of alienation within my immediate family because I knew the pain of being unaccepted. It never occurred to me that alienation does not just come from thinking differently from those you love; it can also come when someone else feels they cannot accept you if you do not agree with his or her way of thinking.

It is important for me also to say that I am profoundly grateful for my husband's parents, who were kind and generous and loved and accepted us to the best of their ability, and I would not be who I am today without the gift of them being who they were in my life. It is a great and valuable gift to surrender what you thought life should have looked like and embrace the path you are on. Allow yourself to grow here and be rooted and grounded where you are planted.

> Dear Kate,
>
> Ask God for wisdom along the way. Many times throughout my life, I have worried about being in the right place. I have come to understand that God is walking beside me each day. There are times when everything is quiet and I do not see him until I look at the path behind me and see his footprints next to mine. This also reminds me of the quote, "The teacher is always quiet during the test." Let this encourage you to walk confidently in God's love. Know that he will suggest a different direction of your steps if it serves you

better. You have looked for him since you were a child; trust that you will know and hear his voice.

When you are unsure of what to do next, ask for directions, and in the meantime, do whatever your job is right now to the best of your ability. Whatever your task on any given day, do your best. I remember hearing a speaker say, "There is a little touch of heaven in the everyday things you do."

When you are making dinner for those you love, this is a gift of love. When doing never-ending loads of laundry for your family, it is a gift of love. When cleaning your home yet again, this is a labor of love. Find joy in the trivial things, for I think you will find that often, what seems like trivial things add up to the most important things.

Look for beauty today. Take time to look around you, look into the eyes of the person next to you, and ask him or her about his or her life. Let this verse be your motto: "And so we know and rely on the love God has for us. God is love. Whoever lives in love lives in God, and God in them" (1 John 4:16, NIV).

You might be tempted to wish you were doing something of greater significance each day. Remember, the world would stop growing or functioning if, for example, suddenly the carpenter could no longer build, the janitor could no longer unplug a toilet, and the cashier, whether a person or automated, could no longer scan your groceries. Each detail that each of us contributes to life is significant.

Kate, have you considered what a joy it is when you receive a delivery from a guy who is whistling as he hands you your box? Have you thought about what a sweet gift it is when a neighbor brings a box meant for you but was delivered to his or her address, and you have a short conversation and realize your neighbor is a kind person? Suddenly your neighborhood feels more welcoming because you know those next to you a little bit better. When each person finds joy in what he or she is doing, the world is a kinder place filled with smiling faces, and you just cannot help but smile back.

Throughout the world, there are millions of women and a variety of life experiences. I know only the one I am personally experiencing, so I will write about what I know, while I also appreciate and honor each woman's individual journey.

We are many individuals, but we have more in common than we know. Let this inspire you to get to know your neighbors and those in your communities. Sharing details with each other about each of our individual journeys enables us to see that those who choose a different path are not as different from us as we might think.

When you are intentional with being in the present moment, there are things you will notice about the people around you that will bring a new beauty to your life, and the things you do each day will suddenly spark joy because you see them through a new lens. At the end of the day, you will feel rewarded for your accomplishments, ordinary though they may be.

I have found that in whatever state I find myself, whether the day is sunny or dreary, taking time to feel gratitude for things exactly as they are, even when incredibly challenging, allows me to find joy in every experience. There are days when feeling grateful does not come easy, but the extra effort to dig until I feel thankful for the things that are good in my life helps take the focus off my problems and enables me to see the many blessings I am gifted with.

When someone comes to your mind, pray for that person and text, call, or write him or her a note or letter. When you see beauty in another person, tell him or her. Share compliments freely, even when you think others might not need to hear what you think. Be bold in loving others. It does not take light away from your candle to light someone else's; in fact, sometimes it causes yours to burn even brighter.

Be happy when you feel it. Allow sadness to wash over you when it wants to come. Allow yourself to be excited without fear of future disappointment. Allow yourself to grieve for the loss of someone's presence because your life was better with that person in it. Cry when tears want to come, because tears are a language too and release emotions having been held within your body. "She is clothed with strength and dignity; she can laugh at the days to come. She speaks with wisdom, and faithful instruction is on her tongue. She watches over the affairs of her household and does not eat the bread of idleness" (Proverbs 31:25–27, NIV).

Kate, you get to choose how you do life. When you find joy in each thing you do, each experience is sweeter. Even when things go sideways, as they often do, and life gets incredibly stressful, remember that also in this, you should take a deep breath and feel gratitude for this moment. You can do it. You were born for such a time as this, for this time, and for this season.

Love, Kate

Printed in the United States
by Baker & Taylor Publisher Services